Cash Flow Circus: The Digital Economy and Online Opportunities

Contents

I0465451

Chapter 1: Introduction to the Digital Economy

1. **The Shift to Digital**

   o   The Evolution of Online Business Models

   o   How Technology is Redefining Work

   o   Benefits and Challenges of Digital Work

2. **The Global Reach of the Digital Economy**

   o   Accessing International Markets

   o   Cross-Border Transactions and Payments

   o   Adapting to Cultural and Economic Differences

3. **The Skills Needed for Digital Success**

   o   Technical Skills vs. Soft Skills

   o   Building a Digital-Ready Mindset

   o   Learning Resources and Platforms

Chapter 2: Making Money Online – Blogging, YouTube, and Social Media

1. **Blogging for Profit**

   - Niche Selection and Content Creation

   - Monetizing Through Ads and Affiliate Marketing

   - SEO and Traffic Growth Strategies

2. **Building a YouTube Channel**

   - Choosing Your Channel's Focus

   - Monetization Methods: Ads, Sponsorships, and Memberships

   - Growing Subscribers and Viewer Engagement

3. **Social Media Influencing and Marketing**

   - Platforms: Instagram, TikTok, Twitter, and More

   - Creating Engaging Content

   - Monetization through Brand Collaborations and Paid Posts

4. **Leveraging Online Courses and Webinars**

   - Creating and Selling Digital Courses

   - Building Authority in Your Niche

   - Using Webinars for Engagement and Sales

Chapter 3: E-Commerce and Dropshipping

1. **Understanding E-Commerce Business Models**
   - Dropshipping, Wholesale, and Private Label
   - Choosing the Right Model for You
   - Managing Logistics and Fulfilment

2. **Setting Up Your E-Commerce Store**
   - Choosing the Right E-Commerce Platform
   - Designing and Customising Your Storefront
   - Integrating Tools and Technologies

3. **Marketing Strategies for E-Commerce Success**
   - Search Engine Optimisation (SEO)
   - Paid Advertising
   - Social Media Marketing

4. **Scaling Your E-commerce Business**
   - Automation and Workflow Optimisation
   - Expanding to International Markets
   - Leveraging Data for Strategic Growth

5. **Building Customer Loyalty in E-Commerce**
   - Creating a Personalised Customer Experience
   - Developing Effective Loyalty Programmes
   - Turning Customers into Brand Advocates

Chapter 4: Cryptocurrency and Blockchain Opportunities

1. **Introduction to Cryptocurrency**

   - What is Cryptocurrency and How It Works

   - Types of Cryptocurrencies and Their Uses

   - Risks and Rewards of Investing in Crypto

2. **Blockchain Beyond Cryptocurrency**

   - Understanding Blockchain Technology

   - Potential Use Cases in Various Industries

   - The Role of Blockchain in Digital Security

3. **Earning Opportunities in the Crypto Space**

   - Staking, Mining, and Yield Farming

   - Participating in Initial Coin Offerings (ICOs) and Token Sales

   - Freelancing and Getting Paid in Cryptocurrency

4. **Risks and Legal Considerations in Crypto**

   - Regulatory Landscape and Compliance

   - Avoiding Scams and Frauds

   - Tax Implications and Reporting

Chapter 5: Freelancing and Remote Work Opportunities

1. **Setting Up a Freelancing Business**

   o Choosing Your Niche and Skillset

   o Platforms for Freelancers (Upwork, Fiverr, etc.)

   o Crafting an Effective Profile and Portfolio

2. **Maximizing Income as a Freelancer**

   o Pricing Strategies and Negotiation Skills

   o Finding High-Paying Clients and Retainers

   o Building Long-Term Client Relationships

3. **Tools and Technologies for Remote Work**

   o Project Management and Communication Tools

   o Collaboration and Cloud-Based Software

   o Staying Productive and Organized Remotely

4. **Freelancing Legal and Financial Considerations**

   o Contracts and Client Agreements

   o Invoicing, Payments, and Taxes

   o Protecting Intellectual Property

Chapter 6: Investment Opportunities in the Digital World

1. **Investing in Digital Real Estate**

   o   Domain Flipping and Website Investments

   o   Virtual Real Estate in the Metaverse

   o   Monetizing Digital Properties

2. **Buying and Selling Websites and Apps**

   o   Platforms for Buying/Selling Websites (Flippa, Empire Flippers)

   o   Valuation Metrics for Digital Assets

   o   Due Diligence and Risk Assessment

3. **Crowdfunding and Peer-to-Peer Lending**

   o   Types of Crowdfunding: Rewards, Equity, and Debt-Based

   o   Risks and Returns of P2P Lending

   o   Crowdfunding Platforms and Opportunities

4. **Passive Income through Digital Investments**

   o   Affiliate Websites and Content Sites

   o   Subscription Models and Membership Sites

   o   Digital Products and E-books

Chapter 7: The Future of Digital Opportunities

1. Emerging Technologies and Trends

- o Artificial Intelligence, VR/AR, and IoT
- o The Growing Role of AI in Digital Business
- o Sustainable and Green Digital Economy Trends

2. Preparing for the Next Digital Revolution

- o Adapting to Rapid Technological Change
- o Building a Future-Proof Skillset
- o Innovation and Creativity in Digital Business

3. Building a Legacy in the Digital Age

- o Planning for Long-Term Financial Stability
- o Creating a Lasting Impact and Brand
- o Digital Estate Planning and Legacy Management

Conclusion: Achieving Success in the Digital Economy

- Summing Up Digital Economy Essentials
- Staying Adaptable and Resilient
- Motivation for Future Growth and Learning

Chapter 1: Introduction to the Digital Economy

The rise of the digital economy is reshaping our world, redefining the way we conduct business, work, and interact with technology. This shift is not just a passing trend but a transformation impacting industries, job roles, and opportunities for wealth creation across the globe. From e-commerce giants in the United States to innovative remote work policies in the UK and the European Union's strict privacy regulations, the digital economy affects every market, region, and individual. To understand its implications, we need to look at how and why this digital evolution began and explore the forces driving this seismic shift.

In this chapter, we will examine the underlying structure of the digital economy, beginning with the evolution of online business models, the role of technology in redefining work, and the unique benefits and challenges that come with these changes. By grasping these fundamentals, individuals and businesses can make informed decisions in this new economic era, whether aiming to launch a startup, navigate remote work, or capitalise on new market opportunities.

1. The Shift to Digital

The shift to digital is the driving force behind the rise of new economic models, from online retail and streaming services to freelancing platforms and blockchain technology. For businesses and individuals alike, adapting to this shift is crucial for maintaining relevance and competitiveness. This transformation is more than the adoption of digital tools; it's a fundamental rethinking of business structures, workflows, and economic strategies. This section explores how the shift to digital has influenced the creation of new business models, redefined work, and introduced both opportunities and challenges on a global scale.

1.1 The Evolution of Online Business Models

The digital economy has enabled the creation of entirely new business models that differ from traditional approaches in profound ways. These models harness the power of technology to reach audiences at an unprecedented scale, offer new ways to deliver value, and allow for an enhanced level of flexibility and customisation. Here, we'll look at three major digital business models that exemplify this evolution: e-commerce, the gig economy, and subscription-based services.

1.1.1 E-commerce and Online Retail

E-commerce has transformed the retail industry, allowing businesses to reach a global audience and making it easier than ever for consumers to shop for products online. This model has seen impressive growth across different regions, influenced by local consumer preferences, regulatory frameworks, and technological infrastructure.

1. **The USA: Leading the E-commerce Revolution**
   The United States has been at the forefront of the e-commerce revolution, driven by pioneering companies like Amazon. Starting as an online bookstore, Amazon quickly expanded into a multi-faceted online marketplace, offering everything from electronics and fashion to groceries and cloud computing services. Its success has reshaped consumer expectations, with customers now expecting fast, reliable, and even same-day delivery. Additionally, the popularity of digital wallets, such as PayPal and Apple Pay, has simplified the purchasing process, reinforcing e-commerce as a primary retail method.

   o **Amazon's Impact on Consumer Behaviour:** The rise of Amazon has led to increased consumer demand for convenience and speed, pushing other retailers to improve their online offerings.

   o **Niche Marketplaces and Specialisation:** Beyond Amazon, niche platforms like Etsy cater to specific markets, including handmade and vintage items, while platforms like Poshmark focus on second-hand and resale fashion.

- o **Rise of Mobile Shopping**: Mobile shopping has become increasingly popular, with consumers using apps to make purchases anytime, anywhere. This trend has led to the optimisation of e-commerce sites for mobile devices.

2. **The UK: Adapting High-Street Retail to Digital Platforms**

In the UK, the transition to online retail has been significant, with high-street brands like Marks & Spencer, ASOS, and Tesco adapting their business models to meet the growing demand for online shopping. British consumers are known for their preference for convenient, mobile-friendly shopping experiences, and the country has a high adoption rate of mobile payments, such as Barclays' Pingit and bPay.

- o **Integration of Click-and-Collect Services**: UK retailers, especially grocery chains, have popularised click-and-collect services, allowing customers to order online and pick up in-store.

- o **Adaptation of Traditional Retailers**: Iconic UK retailers, such as John Lewis, have invested heavily in their online presence, incorporating advanced logistics to offer swift and efficient delivery options.

- o **Emphasis on Cybersecurity**: With a high level of online shopping comes an increased focus on cybersecurity, as consumers demand secure payment methods and data protection.

3. **The European Union: Cross-Border Shopping and Regional Preferences**

The European Union has a diverse e-commerce landscape, with distinct consumer preferences and purchasing habits varying from country to country. The

EU's harmonised regulatory framework supports cross-border e-commerce, allowing businesses to reach a broader audience while adhering to strict privacy and consumer protection standards.

- **Cross-Border E-commerce Growth**: The EU's regulatory environment encourages cross-border sales, making it easier for consumers to shop from neighbouring countries. This has led to the rise of platforms that cater to specific regions, such as Zalando in Germany and Carrefour in France.

- **Regional Variations in Payment Preferences**: Payment methods vary widely across Europe, with options such as Klarna in the Nordics, iDEAL in the Netherlands, and SOFORT in Germany offering tailored solutions for local preferences.

- **GDPR and Data Privacy**: The General Data Protection Regulation (GDPR) has set a global standard for data protection, requiring e-commerce companies to comply with strict rules on consumer data collection and processing.

1.1.2 The Gig Economy and Freelance Platforms

The gig economy represents a shift towards flexible, task-based work, allowing individuals to earn income on their terms. This model has taken root in various industries, from transportation and hospitality to creative services, driven by the desire for flexibility and the accessibility of digital platforms.

1. **USA: Freelancing as a Primary Income Source**
   In the United States, freelancing has grown rapidly, with approximately 36% of the workforce engaged in some form of gig work. Platforms like Upwork, Fiverr, and Uber allow individuals to offer services across a wide range of categories, from digital marketing and graphic design to ridesharing and delivery services.

   o **Rise of Independent Contractors**: Many Americans view freelancing as a viable career path, allowing them to control their schedules and choose projects that align with their skills and interests.

   o **Platform-Specific Niches**: Certain platforms cater to specific fields; for example, Fiverr is popular among creatives, while TaskRabbit focuses on local, hands-on tasks.

   o **Challenges of Healthcare and Retirement Benefits**: Freelancers in the USA face unique challenges, as they must source their own healthcare and retirement benefits, which are traditionally provided by employers.

2. **UK: Freelancing for Flexibility and Work-Life Balance**
   The gig economy has become a popular option in the UK, where many people seek flexible work arrangements. Platforms such as PeoplePerHour and TaskRabbit are commonly used, and the UK government is exploring policies to protect gig workers, ensuring fair wages and access to essential benefits.

- o **Growing Acceptance of Freelancing**:
  Freelancing is increasingly viewed as a
  respectable and sustainable career choice,
  especially in creative fields like writing, design,
  and consulting.

- o **Emphasis on Worker Rights**: The UK has been
  proactive in considering worker protections,
  such as holiday pay and pension contributions,
  for gig workers.

- o **Localised Platforms and Job Opportunities**:
  Beyond global platforms, UK-specific sites like
  YunoJuno cater to freelancers in high-demand
  industries like marketing and project
  management.

3. **Europe: Balancing Flexibility with Worker
   Protections**
   Europe's approach to the gig economy is unique, as the
   EU's focus on workers' rights means that freelancers
   enjoy more robust protections. In countries like France
   and Germany, local platforms, such as Malt, provide
   professional freelancers with work opportunities across
   fields, while ensuring compliance with social protection
   standards.

- o **Worker Rights and Social Protections**:
  European gig workers benefit from stronger
  protections, including access to healthcare,
  pension schemes, and unemployment benefits.

- o **Cultural Attitudes Toward Freelancing**:
  While freelancing is growing in popularity,
  cultural perceptions vary across Europe. In some
  countries, full-time employment is still
  preferred, while others embrace the flexibility
  offered by gig work.

- o **Support for Skills Development**: European
  nations invest in programmes that upskill

freelancers, helping them remain competitive in a dynamic job market.

1.1.3 Subscription-Based and Streaming Services

Subscription-based business models have changed how consumers access products and services, offering convenience and customisation in various industries. From media streaming to software services, subscriptions allow companies to generate recurring revenue and build long-term customer relationships.

1. **USA: Subscription Media and E-commerce Growth**
   In the USA, companies like Netflix, Disney+, and Spotify pioneered the subscription model, particularly in media and entertainment. Subscription e-commerce has also flourished, with brands like Dollar Shave Club and HelloFresh delivering curated product selections to consumers on a regular basis.

   o **Transformation of Media Consumption**: Streaming services have shifted consumer preferences from traditional media ownership to on-demand access.

   o **Subscription Boxes for Every Niche**: Subscription boxes, such as Birchbox and Blue Apron, cater to various interests, providing consumers with curated products in categories like beauty, food, and fashion.

   o **Impact on Consumer Loyalty**: Subscription models foster customer loyalty and retention, as users are more likely to remain subscribed to services that meet their ongoing needs.

2. **UK: Expanding Subscription Services in Media and Software**
   Subscription-based services are on the rise in the UK, with media streaming services like BBC iPlayer and BritBox gaining traction. Additionally, Software as a Service (SaaS) has seen increased adoption among

businesses, providing affordable access to tools for data management, collaboration, and communication.

- o **Growth of SaaS Solutions**: Many UK businesses, particularly startups, rely on SaaS solutions like Microsoft 365 and Salesforce for their daily operations.

- o **Subscription Boxes and Personalisation**: Subscription boxes tailored to British tastes, such as Graze and Bloom & Wild, are increasingly popular, offering everything from snacks to fresh flowers.

- o **Adoption of Fitness and Wellness Subscriptions**: The popularity of fitness subscriptions, such as Peloton and Fiit, highlights a trend toward digital wellness services.

3. **Europe: Localised Subscription Models and Consumer Preferences**
European consumers value subscription services tailored to their local needs and preferences. Platforms like DAZN, a sports streaming service, and Cyberobics, a fitness streaming app, cater to specific European markets, adapting content to regional tastes.

- o **Cultural Tailoring in Subscription Content**: Subscription services in Europe often tailor content to meet cultural preferences, such as region-specific streaming options.

- o **Success of Subscription Boxes**: Subscription boxes for physical goods, such as My Little Box in France, highlight the versatility of this model across different consumer interests.

- o **Challenges of Compliance and Consumer Rights**: European subscription services must navigate complex regulations, such as GDPR, to ensure consumer rights are protected and data is handled responsibly.

1.2 How Technology is Redefining Work

Technology has not only introduced new business models; it has fundamentally redefined work itself. Digital tools and advancements now shape where and how we work, the types of roles that are available, and the skills needed for success. This redefinition of work is unfolding at various speeds across regions, influenced by factors like technological infrastructure, workplace culture, and government policies.

1.2.1 Remote Work and the Hybrid Model

The shift to remote work, accelerated by the COVID-19 pandemic, has transformed traditional office culture and introduced the hybrid model—a blend of in-office and remote work that offers flexibility for employees and cost savings for employers. While each region has adapted to remote work differently, the trend towards flexible work environments is global.

1. **USA: Leading Remote Work Trends in Tech and Finance**
   In the USA, major technology companies like Twitter, Facebook, and Google were some of the first to adopt long-term remote work policies. As they did, businesses across various sectors began following suit, with the hybrid model emerging as a preferred approach in industries like finance, technology, and professional services. However, these changes bring both opportunities and challenges.

   o **The Rise of Permanent Remote Positions**: Many companies in the tech sector now offer permanent remote roles, recognising that talent is no longer limited by geographic location.

- o **Hybrid Work Models in Financial Services**: Financial institutions, traditionally office-centric, are adopting hybrid work policies to retain talent while minimising office costs.

- o **Productivity and Mental Health**: Employers are investing in digital wellness tools to monitor and support employee productivity and mental health, as remote work blurs work-life boundaries.

2. **UK: Nationwide Shift to Flexible Work Arrangements**
   In the UK, remote work became widespread during the pandemic, particularly in sectors like finance, technology, and education. As a result, British companies are increasingly adopting hybrid work arrangements, supported by government guidelines that encourage flexible working practices.

   - o **Government Guidelines and Support**: The UK government actively promotes flexible work policies, recognising their potential to improve work-life balance and productivity.

   - o **Impacts on SMEs and Startups**: Small and medium-sized enterprises (SMEs) have embraced remote work to reduce overheads and access a wider talent pool, making it easier for startups to compete.

   - o **Challenges of Remote Infrastructure**: Despite high adoption rates, some SMEs face challenges with remote work infrastructure, such as cybersecurity and reliable internet access.

3. **Europe: A Varied Approach to Flexibility and Work-Life Balance**
   Europe's approach to remote work is diverse, with each country adapting in ways that reflect its labour culture and regulatory environment. Countries like Germany and the Netherlands have embraced flexible work policies,

while southern European nations, such as Italy and Spain, are transitioning at a slower pace.

- **France's Labour Laws on Remote Work**: France has adopted specific regulations that support remote workers' rights, including mandatory breaks and measures to prevent burnout.

- **Scandinavia's Focus on Work-Life Balance**: Scandinavian countries, known for prioritising work-life balance, were early adopters of flexible working arrangements, using remote work to enhance employee well-being.

- **Digital Infrastructure Challenges in Rural Areas**: In less urbanised areas of Europe, remote work adoption can be hindered by limited internet infrastructure, highlighting the need for regional investment in digital connectivity.

1.2.2 Automation and Artificial Intelligence

Automation and artificial intelligence (AI) are reshaping job roles across industries, with an emphasis on enhancing productivity, reducing errors, and freeing employees from repetitive tasks. These technologies have different applications across regions, reflecting local workforce dynamics, industry specialisations, and regulatory standards.

1. **USA: Leading Innovation in Automation and AI**
   The USA is a global leader in automation and AI, with sectors like healthcare, manufacturing, and finance integrating these technologies to improve efficiency and service quality. In healthcare, AI is used for diagnostics and patient management, while finance relies on AI for risk analysis and fraud prevention.

   - **Healthcare Innovation through AI**: AI-powered tools are transforming patient diagnostics, using predictive analytics to improve accuracy and efficiency in identifying health risks.

- o **Manufacturing and Robotic Process Automation (RPA)**: The manufacturing sector has widely adopted RPA, allowing companies to streamline production processes and maintain quality control.

- o **Reskilling and Upskilling**: Recognising the potential for job displacement, many organisations are offering training programmes to help employees transition to roles that require more complex problem-solving and AI management skills.

2. **UK: Expanding AI Adoption in Public and Private Sectors**

   In the UK, AI and automation are being integrated across various industries, with both private companies and government agencies investing in these technologies. The healthcare sector, in particular, has benefited from AI, with applications in diagnostics, scheduling, and patient management.

   - o **AI in Public Health Initiatives**: The UK's National Health Service (NHS) uses AI for predictive healthcare, aiming to reduce waiting times and improve patient outcomes.

   - o **Investment in Corporate AI**: Leading UK businesses are investing heavily in AI to improve operational efficiency and customer service, with sectors like banking and telecommunications leading the way.

   - o **Training and Skill Development**: To address concerns over job automation, the UK government provides funding for AI-related training, ensuring workers are prepared for a more automated job market.

3. **Europe: Emphasising Ethical AI and Workforce Adaptation**

   Europe's approach to automation and AI balances innovation with ethical considerations. The European Union has proposed regulations to govern the responsible use of AI, focusing on transparency, data protection, and avoiding bias.

   o **The EU's Regulatory Framework for AI**: Proposed EU regulations aim to create a standardised approach to AI, ensuring that AI systems are safe, transparent, and ethical.

   o **Industry-Specific AI Adoption**: Europe's automotive sector has widely adopted AI for tasks like predictive maintenance and quality control, enhancing productivity while reducing human error.

   o **Upskilling Initiatives for Job Transition**: European countries invest in training programmes for workers affected by automation, focusing on digital skills that prepare them for high-demand roles in data analysis, cybersecurity, and AI development.

1.2.3 Collaborative Tools and Cloud Technology

The rise of cloud-based collaboration tools has transformed how teams communicate and manage projects, particularly in the age of remote and hybrid work. Cloud technology allows for real-time data access, flexible storage, and seamless project collaboration, making it essential for modern work environments.

1. **USA: Growth in Cloud and Collaborative Solutions**

   In the USA, cloud-based collaboration tools like Google Workspace, Microsoft Teams, and Slack have become standard for remote and in-office teams alike. Cloud technology is particularly valuable in industries that require constant communication and data sharing, such as technology, media, and finance.

- **Adoption in Large Enterprises**: Major corporations use cloud solutions to manage large volumes of data, with applications in customer relationship management, inventory tracking, and supply chain logistics.

- **Security and Privacy Concerns**: As reliance on cloud technology grows, companies are investing in cybersecurity measures to protect sensitive data from breaches.

- **Flexible Work Benefits**: Cloud tools support flexible work arrangements, allowing employees to access files and collaborate from any location, enhancing productivity and work-life balance.

2. **UK: Digital Transformation and Cloud Uptake in Public Services**
   The UK government has actively encouraged the adoption of cloud technology in public services, using it to improve efficiency and data management. Private companies, especially in sectors like finance and retail, have also widely adopted cloud solutions to optimise operations.

   - **Government Cloud Initiatives**: Public sector organisations use cloud-based systems to streamline operations, manage data securely, and reduce paperwork.

   - **Remote Collaboration in SMEs**: Small and medium-sized enterprises (SMEs) use tools like Zoom, Slack, and Trello to facilitate remote work and manage projects efficiently.

   - **Focus on Data Compliance**: The UK's Data Protection Act, in alignment with GDPR, requires companies to implement stringent data protection measures in cloud environments.

3. **Europe: Cross-Border Collaboration and Localised Cloud Providers**

   Europe's diverse languages and regulatory requirements necessitate cloud solutions that accommodate cross-border collaboration. European companies often opt for region-specific cloud providers that comply with GDPR and meet local needs.

   - **Cloud Solutions for Multinational Teams**: Cloud technology enables seamless collaboration across different countries, allowing team members to work on shared projects in real time.

   - **Preference for GDPR-Compliant Providers**: European businesses frequently choose local cloud providers like OVHcloud and T-Systems to ensure data protection compliance.

   - **Public Sector Cloud Adoption**: Many EU countries, including Germany and France, use cloud technology to improve public service efficiency, with applications in healthcare, education, and government administration.

1.3 Benefits and Challenges of Digital Work

Digital work provides numerous advantages, including increased flexibility, opportunities for skill development, and access to a global job market. However, it also presents challenges that require careful consideration, such as data privacy, job security, and work-life balance. This section examines the benefits and challenges associated with digital work, offering insights for individuals and businesses navigating the evolving workplace.

1.3.1 Flexibility and Work-Life Balance

One of the most attractive aspects of digital work is the flexibility it offers, allowing employees to customise their schedules and balance personal and professional commitments. However, this flexibility can blur the lines between work and personal life, posing challenges for work-life balance.

1. **USA: Shifting Work-Life Boundaries in Remote Work**
   In the USA, the rise of remote work has led to significant changes in work-life boundaries. Many companies have adopted flexible scheduling policies, but some employees struggle to disconnect from work due to the "always-on" culture.

   o **Company Policies on Disconnecting**: Some companies are implementing policies that encourage employees to set boundaries, such as "no meeting" days or email curfews.

   o **Use of Digital Wellness Tools**: Wellness apps and programs, such as Headspace for Work, help employees manage stress and mental health.

   o **Impact on Job Satisfaction**: Studies show that flexible work options can improve job satisfaction, though setting clear boundaries remains essential for long-term success.

2. **UK: Emphasis on Flexibility and Mental Health**
   In the UK, flexibility is increasingly valued, with many employees prioritising work-life balance over traditional career advancement. British companies are responding by offering flexible work arrangements and supporting mental health initiatives.

   o **Mental Health Resources in the Workplace**: UK employers are investing in mental health resources, including counselling services and employee assistance programmes (EAPs).

   o **Flexible Working Rights**: UK law allows employees to request flexible work arrangements, empowering them to structure work around their needs.

   o **Wellness Programmes and Support**: Companies are providing wellness programmes to help employees maintain balance and prevent burnout.

3. **Europe: Balancing Flexibility with Cultural Norms**
   European countries have long prioritised work-life balance, with cultural norms supporting shorter work hours and extensive leave policies. The shift to digital work has reinforced this focus, allowing for even greater flexibility.

   o **Scandinavia's Flexible Work Hours**: Scandinavian countries, such as Sweden and Denmark, allow employees to structure their work hours flexibly, supporting a healthy balance.

   o **Remote Work in the EU**: The EU promotes flexible work through policies that prioritise well-being, and companies in countries like France and the Netherlands offer remote work options as standard.

- o **Focus on Family and Personal Time**: European culture places a high value on family time, with work policies reflecting a commitment to personal well-being.

1.3.2 Increased Opportunities for Skill Development

The digital economy has brought unprecedented access to skill development resources, enabling workers worldwide to upskill, reskill, and remain competitive in rapidly evolving industries. This shift has provided opportunities for professional growth across regions and industries, though it also presents the challenge of staying current in a constantly changing job market.

1. **USA: Demand for Technical and Soft Skills**
   In the USA, the rise of digital work has led to increased demand for technical skills in fields like coding, data analysis, and digital marketing, as well as soft skills like communication and adaptability. Many professionals are turning to online learning platforms to acquire these skills, with corporate support to help meet industry demands.

   - o **Corporate Support for Upskilling**: Many large corporations offer employees access to LinkedIn Learning, Coursera, and other online platforms to support skill development and career advancement.

   - o **Tech Skills in High Demand**: Skills in data science, artificial intelligence, and cybersecurity are especially valuable, with companies willing to invest in upskilling employees in these areas.

   - o **Reskilling for Non-Tech Roles**: Even in non-technical fields, digital literacy is essential. Programmes focused on customer service, project management, and sales training now often incorporate digital tools and analytics.

2. **UK: Emphasis on Lifelong Learning and Government Initiatives**
    The UK has a strong tradition of lifelong learning, supported by government-backed initiatives and professional development schemes. This emphasis on continuous education has encouraged workers to pursue training and certification in areas like technology, management, and healthcare.

    o   **Apprenticeships and Professional Certifications**: The UK government supports a wide range of apprenticeships and certifications, helping workers gain practical skills alongside theoretical knowledge.

    o   **Digital Literacy for All**: Digital skills are increasingly essential across all roles, prompting an emphasis on making digital literacy accessible, even for those in traditionally non-digital jobs.

    o   **Workforce Retraining for Digital Transformation**: Government programmes and partnerships with educational institutions focus on upskilling workers to fill gaps in critical fields like healthcare, digital marketing, and software development.

3. **Europe: Preparing the Workforce for Digital Transformation**
    The EU has implemented initiatives to support digital literacy and workforce adaptation, focusing on high-demand skills that align with Europe's future economic priorities. European countries often subsidise training and educational programmes to promote skill development across industries.

    o   **EU Digital Skills and Jobs Coalition**: This initiative provides resources for digital training and supports partnerships that address skill shortages in areas like ICT (Information and Communication Technology).

- o **Industry-Specific Training**: EU nations have tailored training programmes for sectors such as green technology, automotive, and manufacturing, where digital tools and processes are increasingly essential.

- o **Lifelong Learning and University Partnerships**: Many European countries have formed partnerships between universities and industries, ensuring that the workforce is equipped with relevant skills in fields like AI, robotics, and clean energy.

1.3.3 Challenges of Job Security and Social Isolation

While digital work offers flexibility, it also brings unique challenges. Freelancers and gig workers often face income instability, lack of benefits, and limited job security. Additionally, remote and freelance work can create a sense of social isolation, as workers miss out on in-person interactions with colleagues.

1. **USA: Financial Instability and Lack of Benefits**
   In the USA, where health insurance and retirement benefits are often tied to traditional employment, gig and freelance workers face unique challenges. Without the safety net of employer-provided benefits, freelancers must independently manage their finances and secure necessary protections.

   - o **Income Variability and Job Security**: Many gig workers experience fluctuating income, making it difficult to plan for the long term. As demand for gig work can be seasonal, financial planning is essential.

   - o **Self-Managed Healthcare and Retirement**: Freelancers are responsible for their own

27

healthcare and retirement plans, often turning to marketplaces or associations that provide options at reduced rates.

- o **Mental Health and Social Isolation**: Working independently can lead to feelings of isolation, with freelancers missing the social structure and support networks of traditional workplaces.

2. **UK: Employment Rights and Freelancer Protections**
   The UK has taken steps to address freelancer rights, with discussions surrounding the extension of certain protections, such as paid leave and pension contributions, to gig workers. However, freelancers and remote workers still face challenges related to financial security and social isolation.

   - o **Progressive Worker Rights for Gig Workers**: The UK government is exploring legislation to provide benefits for freelancers, including minimum wage protections and paid sick leave.

   - o **Retirement Savings for Freelancers**: The lack of employer-sponsored pensions means freelancers must set aside income for retirement, often through self-invested personal pensions (SIPPs).

   - o **Support Networks and Co-Working Spaces**: To counter isolation, many freelancers use co-working spaces and professional networks, providing a sense of community and connection with like-minded professionals.

3. **Europe: Addressing Security and Social Well-Being**
   European countries have strong social safety nets, providing gig workers and freelancers with better access to benefits and protections. Countries like Germany and France offer freelancers options for healthcare, unemployment benefits, and retirement plans, while promoting mental health initiatives.

o **Social Protections for Freelancers**: Many European countries have extended social protections to gig workers, allowing them to access healthcare, pensions, and other benefits similar to traditional employees.

o **Unemployment Benefits for Freelancers**: In countries like France, freelancers can access unemployment benefits under certain conditions, helping to mitigate financial insecurity during slow periods.

o **Mental Health Resources and Community Initiatives**: European governments and professional networks offer resources for mental well-being, and co-working spaces provide a social outlet for remote and freelance workers.

Conclusion

The digital economy is transforming the global business landscape, creating opportunities and challenges across all aspects of work and industry. As businesses and individuals adapt to this new economic reality, understanding the evolution of online business models, the changing nature of work, and the benefits and challenges of digitalisation is essential.

For entrepreneurs and businesses, digitalisation offers unprecedented opportunities to reach new markets, streamline operations, and build resilient models. For individuals, it introduces flexibility, learning opportunities, and access to global job markets, though it also requires self-management and adaptability in areas like financial planning, mental health, and skill development.

This foundational chapter sets the stage for exploring these themes in greater depth. In the following chapters, we will delve into specific digital economy opportunities, from e-commerce and content creation to cryptocurrency and blockchain, providing the tools needed to succeed in this dynamic environment.

2. The Global Reach of the Digital Economy

The digital economy has enabled unprecedented global connectivity, allowing businesses and individuals to reach international markets with ease. This global reach has opened new revenue streams, enabled the exchange of ideas, and driven economic growth across borders. However, navigating the international digital landscape requires an understanding of regional markets, the mechanics of cross-border transactions, and the cultural nuances that impact business. In this section, we will explore how businesses are accessing international markets, handling cross-border payments, and adapting to diverse cultural and economic environments.

2.1 Accessing International Markets

Accessing international markets is one of the biggest advantages of the digital economy. Digital platforms and online business models allow companies of all sizes to reach customers globally, removing the need for physical presence in each market. This subsection will explore the strategies and considerations involved in entering new markets digitally, highlighting specific practices in the USA, UK, Europe, and globally.

2.1.1 Market Research and Localisation Strategies

Understanding the target market is crucial for any business looking to expand internationally. Market research and localisation strategies help businesses tailor their offerings to meet the preferences and expectations of different regions.

1. **USA: Competitive Market Insights**
   The USA is a highly competitive market, with consumer preferences that vary by region, age, and socioeconomic background. Conducting market research is essential to understand these preferences, and localisation goes beyond translation to include adapting products, services, and marketing to align with American cultural expectations.

- o **Market Analysis Tools**: Tools like Nielsen, Google Trends, and Statista provide businesses with insights into American consumer behaviour and emerging trends.

- o **Adapting to Regional Preferences**: The USA's vast geography means preferences can vary widely; for example, health and eco-conscious products are in high demand in states like California, while convenience and affordability may be more prioritised in other regions.

- o **Influencer Marketing**: Partnering with local influencers is an effective way for international brands to connect with American consumers and build trust.

2. **UK: Localisation and Consumer Trust**

   The UK market values quality, trust, and familiarity. British consumers are responsive to brands that feel "local" and trustworthy, even when they originate from abroad. Effective localisation and strong customer service are key to gaining traction in the UK.

   - o **Language and Tone**: While UK English is distinct from American English, localisation efforts must also consider cultural nuances, such as humour and preferences for formal or informal tone.

   - o **Emphasis on Quality and Value**: UK consumers tend to prioritise quality and value, particularly in e-commerce. Brands must highlight these aspects to appeal to British shoppers.

   - o **Brand Partnerships**: Partnering with established UK brands or retailers can help international companies gain trust and increase brand recognition.

3. **Europe: Cultural Diversity and Regulatory Requirements**

Europe is not a monolithic market, with each country exhibiting unique cultural and regulatory characteristics. Localisation efforts must consider the diverse languages, preferences, and legal requirements across the region.

- o **Language Adaptation and Multilingual Websites**: Offering multilingual options is critical in Europe, where consumers are more likely to engage with content in their native language. Brands often need language-specific sites for countries like Germany, France, and Spain.

- o **Adapting to Regional Values**: European consumers tend to prioritise environmental sustainability and ethical business practices, making these elements important to emphasise in marketing strategies.

- o **Navigating the EU's Legal Landscape**: Compliance with EU regulations, such as GDPR, is essential for international businesses operating in Europe. Understanding data privacy laws and e-commerce guidelines helps companies avoid legal issues and build consumer trust.

2.1.2 Digital Marketing and Social Media Strategy

Digital marketing and social media are essential for building brand awareness in new markets. Effective strategies take into account regional trends, platform preferences, and local influencers, allowing brands to engage audiences in a way that feels authentic and relevant.

1. **USA: Social Media as a Primary Marketing Tool**

Social media is a dominant marketing platform in the USA, with platforms like Instagram, Facebook, and TikTok being essential for reaching American consumers. Businesses must develop strategies tailored to the fast-paced, visual nature of these platforms.

- o **Influencer Collaborations**: Partnering with American influencers, from celebrities to micro-influencers, can help brands quickly gain visibility and credibility.

- o **Targeted Advertising**: Tools like Facebook Ads and Google Ads allow for precise targeting, making it possible to reach specific demographics and interests within the USA.

- o **Content Adaptation for Trends**: American social media trends shift quickly, requiring brands to stay current with popular themes and formats, such as short-form video and interactive posts.

2. **UK: Emphasis on Transparency and Engagement**
   British consumers appreciate transparency and authenticity, and brands that engage meaningfully with their audience can build strong loyalty. Social media platforms like Instagram, Twitter, and LinkedIn are widely used for marketing in the UK.

   - o **Transparency in Advertising**: UK consumers value clear, honest advertising. Brands should avoid over-promising or appearing too aggressive in marketing tactics.

   - o **Engagement Through Storytelling**: British audiences respond well to storytelling that aligns with their values and interests, whether in lifestyle, sustainability, or local culture.

   - o **Platform-Specific Content**: LinkedIn is particularly effective for B2B marketing in the UK, while Instagram and Facebook are popular for reaching broader consumer audiences.

3. **Europe: Adapting to Regional Preferences and Platform Use**

Digital marketing in Europe must account for regional preferences in platform use and content style. European consumers value privacy and often prefer platforms that offer transparency and data protection.

- o **Platform Diversity**: Social media use varies by country; for instance, Instagram is popular in Southern Europe, while LinkedIn and Xing are widely used in professional circles in Germany.

- o **Localised Content**: Content should reflect local values, with a focus on social responsibility, environmental consciousness, and cultural nuances.

- o **Respect for Data Privacy**: GDPR compliance in digital marketing is non-negotiable in Europe. Brands must clearly communicate data usage policies and obtain consent for targeted advertising.

2.1.3 E-commerce and Logistics Considerations

E-commerce allows businesses to reach international customers directly, but success requires careful planning around logistics, customer service, and regulatory compliance. Each region has unique expectations around delivery speed, return policies, and customer support.

1. **USA: High Expectations for Speed and Convenience** American consumers have come to expect fast, convenient delivery options. E-commerce success in the USA requires logistics that can meet these high standards, often through partnerships with established delivery networks.

   - o **Same-Day and Next-Day Delivery**: Same-day or next-day delivery options, pioneered by Amazon, have become standard in many parts of the USA, especially in urban areas.

   - o **Efficient Returns and Refunds**: A seamless return policy is crucial for building consumer trust; American shoppers expect a straightforward and often free return process.

- o **Customer Service Expectations**: American customers value accessible and responsive customer service, whether through live chat, phone support, or social media interactions.

2. **UK: Focus on Reliability and Sustainable Practices**
   In the UK, consumers appreciate reliable, eco-friendly delivery options. E-commerce brands are expected to offer dependable shipping and demonstrate environmental responsibility in their logistics practices.

   - o **Flexible Delivery Options**: Many UK consumers prefer flexible delivery services, including click-and-collect options and scheduled deliveries that accommodate their lifestyles.

   - o **Eco-Friendly Packaging**: Environmental consciousness is high in the UK, and consumers appreciate brands that minimise plastic use and offer recyclable or biodegradable packaging.

   - o **Transparent Shipping Costs**: UK shoppers are accustomed to clear pricing, and hidden shipping costs can lead to cart abandonment. Displaying total costs upfront is essential.

3. **Europe: Navigating Diverse Delivery Standards and Regulations**

   E-commerce in Europe is shaped by a mix of delivery expectations and regulatory standards across countries. Businesses must navigate varied shipping standards, customer preferences, and legal requirements.

   o **Cross-Border Shipping Solutions**: Efficient cross-border logistics are key, as many European consumers shop from neighbouring countries. Partnerships with reliable carriers like DHL, UPS, and regional postal services help ensure timely delivery.

   o **Return and Refund Requirements**: European consumer rights laws often mandate generous return policies, making it important for businesses to align with local regulations.

   o **Adhering to Import and Export Rules**: Certain products are subject to import and export restrictions in the EU. Brands must understand these rules to avoid delays or legal issues in shipping.

2.2 Cross-Border Transactions and Payments

Conducting cross-border transactions is essential for businesses operating in the digital economy, enabling companies to engage with international customers and expand their reach. However, managing these transactions requires careful planning around currency exchange rates, payment security, and regulatory compliance. This section explores the methods and challenges of cross-border payments, focusing on the complexities faced by businesses in the USA, UK, and Europe.

2.2.1 Currency Exchange and Conversion Rates

Currency exchange is a key consideration for cross-border transactions. For businesses and consumers alike, fluctuations in exchange rates can impact transaction costs, affecting pricing and profitability. Companies must navigate these fluctuations carefully to maintain competitive pricing in international markets.

1. **USA: Dollar Dominance and Exchange Stability**
   The US dollar is a dominant global currency, often used as a standard in international transactions. However, exchange rate fluctuations still impact American businesses trading internationally, particularly when dealing with economies where currency values are more volatile.

   o **Mitigating Exchange Rate Risk**: American companies often use financial tools, such as forward contracts or options, to hedge against exchange rate volatility.

   o **Dual-Currency Pricing**: To make international purchases easier, many US businesses offer pricing in both USD and the local currency of the target market.

   o **Currency Conversion Fees**: Many payment providers charge conversion fees, so businesses must consider these costs to avoid passing excessive charges onto customers.

2. **UK: Pound Sterling and Brexit Implications**
   In the UK, currency exchange has been significantly influenced by Brexit, leading to greater fluctuations in the value of the pound sterling against other currencies. This volatility requires UK businesses to remain agile in managing exchange rates for cross-border transactions.

   o **Currency Volatility and Pricing Strategy**: Brexit-related uncertainties have made the pound more volatile. UK companies must frequently review pricing strategies to account for exchange rate changes.

- ○ **Using Payment Providers with Low Conversion Fees**: Many UK businesses partner with international payment providers that offer competitive exchange rates and minimal conversion fees to make transactions cost-effective.

- ○ **Dynamic Currency Conversion**: Some UK businesses provide customers the option to pay in their preferred currency, reducing the impact of currency fluctuations on the customer's end.

3. **Europe: Euro Stability and Multi-Currency Management**
While the euro is relatively stable within the EU, European businesses working with non-eurozone countries must manage currency conversions carefully. Companies operating across multiple European countries may also need to handle multiple currencies to accommodate regional preferences.

- ○ **Multi-Currency Pricing**: European e-commerce platforms often display prices in multiple currencies, allowing consumers to view costs in their local currency.

- ○ **Currency Hedging in Cross-Border Trade**: To protect against currency risk, businesses use currency hedging strategies, which can help stabilise costs when working across fluctuating currencies.

- ○ **Navigating Exchange Rate Fluctuations in Eastern Europe**: In non-eurozone countries like Poland and Hungary, local currencies can be more volatile, so companies must closely monitor exchange rates to maintain competitive pricing.

2.2.2 International Payment Methods and Processing

Choosing the right payment methods for international transactions is essential for businesses looking to appeal to a global audience. Different regions have varying preferences for payment methods, so understanding these preferences is crucial for maximising sales and customer satisfaction.

1. **USA: Credit Cards and Digital Wallets**
   In the USA, credit cards are the most popular payment method for online purchases, with digital wallets like PayPal, Apple Pay, and Google Wallet also widely accepted. Businesses must consider these preferences to ensure a smooth payment experience for American customers.

   - **Credit Card Acceptance**: Most American consumers expect to use credit cards for online purchases, making it important for international businesses to offer this option.

   - **Integrating Digital Wallets**: Digital wallets provide an added layer of security and convenience, making them attractive to consumers. Many businesses integrate PayPal or Apple Pay for ease of use.

   - **Buy Now, Pay Later (BNPL) Options**: BNPL options, such as Affirm and Klarna, are growing in popularity in the USA. Adding these options can increase accessibility and appeal to younger consumers.

2. **UK: Debit Cards and Local Payment Solutions**
   In the UK, debit cards are the most commonly used payment method, though digital wallets and local solutions like Pay by Bank are also popular. UK consumers value transparency and convenience in payment processing.

- o **Emphasis on Debit Card Usage**: Many UK consumers prefer debit over credit cards, so offering debit card options is essential for appealing to this audience.

- o **Bank Transfer Options**: Services like Pay by Bank allow direct transfers from bank accounts, which are favoured by UK consumers for their simplicity and security.

- o **PayPal and Digital Wallet Integration**: PayPal is widely used in the UK for online transactions, so businesses targeting UK customers often integrate this option into their payment systems.

3. **Europe: Diverse Payment Preferences Across Countries**

   Payment preferences in Europe vary widely by country, with local payment methods often preferred over global solutions. Businesses targeting European consumers must consider these regional preferences to maximise their reach.

   - o **Germany's SOFORT and Giropay**: In Germany, many consumers prefer SOFORT and Giropay, both of which allow direct bank transfers. Offering these options can increase appeal in the German market.

   - o **iDEAL in the Netherlands**: Dutch consumers frequently use iDEAL, a payment method that links to local bank accounts, providing a secure and straightforward payment option.

   - o **France's Carte Bancaire**: In France, Carte Bancaire is commonly used for transactions, so businesses targeting French consumers should consider accepting this option for smoother transactions.

2.2.3 Regulatory Compliance and Payment Security

Compliance with regulatory standards is crucial for cross-border payments. Businesses must adhere to local regulations around data security, anti-fraud measures, and tax implications to ensure secure and lawful transactions in international markets.

1. **USA: Federal Compliance and Anti-Fraud Measures**
   The USA has specific regulations governing online transactions, including compliance requirements for data protection, anti-money laundering (AML), and fraud prevention. Businesses must follow these rules to avoid penalties and maintain customer trust.

   - **PCI DSS Compliance**: Payment Card Industry Data Security Standard (PCI DSS) compliance is mandatory for businesses handling credit card payments, ensuring secure transactions.

   - **AML and KYC Requirements**: Anti-Money Laundering (AML) and Know Your Customer (KYC) laws require businesses to verify customer identities, particularly for large transactions, to prevent financial fraud.

   - **Fraud Detection Tools**: American businesses often use advanced fraud detection tools, such as AI-driven analysis, to identify suspicious activity and protect customer data.

2. **UK: Data Privacy and Secure Payment Processing**
   The UK enforces strict data privacy laws under the Data Protection Act, and businesses must comply with these standards to protect customer information during transactions. Additionally, the UK government encourages the use of secure payment methods to prevent fraud.

   - **GDPR and Data Protection Act Compliance**: The UK's Data Protection Act aligns with GDPR, requiring businesses to handle customer data responsibly and securely.

- o **Strong Customer Authentication (SCA)**: The UK requires Strong Customer Authentication for online payments, adding an extra layer of security through multi-factor authentication.

- o **Integration of Fraud Prevention Tools**: To meet regulatory standards, UK businesses integrate fraud detection tools like address verification and transaction monitoring into their payment systems.

3. **Europe: GDPR and Cross-Border Payment Regulations**

   The EU's GDPR is one of the most stringent data privacy regulations, affecting how businesses handle and protect customer data. Compliance with GDPR is essential for companies conducting cross-border transactions within the EU.

   - o **GDPR Compliance in Payment Processing**: GDPR mandates that businesses process customer data transparently and securely, with clear consent required for data use in payments.

   - o **PSD2 and Payment Security**: The Payment Services Directive 2 (PSD2) requires Strong Customer Authentication (SCA) for online payments, ensuring that transactions are authorised by the customer.

   - o **Cross-Border Tax Compliance**: The EU requires businesses to comply with VAT and other tax regulations when selling across borders, necessitating proper record-keeping and tax reporting.

2.3 Adapting to Cultural and Economic Differences

Cultural and economic differences can have a profound impact on how products and services are received in international markets. From communication styles and marketing preferences

43

to price sensitivity and economic stability, these factors influence how customers perceive brands and make purchasing decisions. Successful international businesses understand these differences and adapt their strategies to meet the needs of each region.

2.3.1 Cultural Sensitivity in Marketing and Branding

Marketing strategies that work in one country may not resonate—or may even backfire—in another due to cultural nuances. Understanding local customs, values, and preferences is essential for creating effective marketing campaigns and building a positive brand image.

1. **USA: Individualism and Direct Communication**
    American culture values individualism, directness, and efficiency. Brands that are straightforward and transparent in their messaging tend to succeed in the USA, where consumers appreciate clear information about product benefits and features.

    o   **Direct Marketing Tactics**: Direct advertising and clear calls to action resonate with American consumers, who appreciate straightforward information about product benefits.

    o   **Value on Customer Experience**: American consumers expect high levels of customer service. Brands that emphasise customer experience and offer responsive support build loyalty.

    o   **Celebrity and Influencer Endorsements**: The USA is a leading market for influencer marketing, with celebrity endorsements adding credibility and appeal to products and services.

2. **UK: Subtlety and Quality-Focused Messaging**
    British culture tends to favour subtlety, with consumers often valuing quality, reliability, and understated marketing. Brands in the UK benefit from a more refined

approach, avoiding overly aggressive or exaggerated claims.

- o **Understated Advertising**: British consumers prefer ads that are informative without being overly pushy. Brands that communicate quality and value without exaggeration are more likely to build trust.

- o **Focus on Quality and Durability**: Emphasising the quality and durability of products appeals to British shoppers, who often view purchasing as an investment rather than an impulse.

- o **Humour in Advertising**: British audiences appreciate humour, especially in advertisements. Witty, clever marketing that reflects local humour can help brands build rapport with UK consumers.

3. **Europe: Diversity and Respect for Local Values**
   Europe is a culturally diverse region with varying consumer preferences. Brands that succeed in Europe often tailor their strategies to reflect the distinct values, traditions, and languages of each country.

   - o **Multilingual Advertising**: Advertising in local languages, rather than solely relying on English, helps build connections with European consumers and demonstrates respect for local culture.

   - o **Focus on Sustainability**: European consumers place a high value on sustainability and social responsibility. Brands that showcase eco-friendly practices and ethical sourcing are well received.

   - o **Local Influences on Design and Aesthetics**: Design preferences vary across Europe. For example, Scandinavian countries prefer minimalist design, while Southern European countries may appreciate more vibrant aesthetics.

2.3.2 Economic Sensitivity and Pricing Strategy

Economic conditions and income levels vary greatly across regions, affecting consumer purchasing power and price sensitivity. To succeed in international markets, businesses must adapt their pricing strategies to align with local economic realities.

1. **USA: Competitive Pricing and Consumer Choice**
   The USA is a highly competitive market, where consumers have access to a wide range of products and services at various price points. Price sensitivity varies across demographics, with many consumers expecting good value for money.

   - **Offering Multiple Pricing Tiers**: Offering products at different price points can help businesses appeal to a wider audience, from budget-conscious shoppers to premium buyers.

   - **Discounts and Promotions**: American consumers respond well to discounts, seasonal sales, and promotional offers, which can boost brand visibility and drive sales.

   - **Subscription Models**: Subscriptions are popular in the USA, as they offer predictable costs and convenience. Businesses may consider offering subscription options as part of their pricing strategy.

2. **UK: Emphasis on Value and Long-Term Investment**
   UK consumers value quality and are often willing to pay more for products they perceive as durable and reliable. Pricing strategies that reflect quality and long-term value tend to be effective in the UK.

- o **Highlighting Value for Money**: Emphasising the quality, craftsmanship, or longevity of products helps justify higher price points for UK consumers.

- o **Transparent Pricing**: UK shoppers appreciate transparency in pricing, with a preference for upfront costs over hidden fees or surcharges.

- o **Budget-Friendly Alternatives**: Offering budget-friendly product ranges or payment plans can attract more price-sensitive segments, making the brand accessible to a wider audience.

3. **Europe: Adapting to Varied Economic Conditions**
   Europe's diverse economies require tailored pricing strategies. While some countries, like Germany and France, have high purchasing power, others may be more price-sensitive due to economic constraints.

   - o **Country-Specific Pricing**: Brands may use regional pricing strategies to align with local income levels, offering lower prices in less affluent markets.

   - o **Payment Plans and Financing Options**: Offering financing options or instalment plans makes products more accessible to consumers in price-sensitive regions.

   - o **Promoting Eco-Friendly and Premium Products**: European consumers often prioritise eco-friendly products, even at higher price points. Highlighting sustainability can make premium products more appealing.

2.3.3 Navigating Local Regulations and Compliance

Local regulations impact nearly every aspect of international business, from data protection and advertising standards to health and safety regulations. Compliance with these regulations is crucial for maintaining brand reputation and avoiding legal challenges.

1. **USA: State and Federal Regulations**
    In the USA, businesses must navigate a complex web of federal and state regulations. Compliance with standards such as the FTC's advertising guidelines, the ADA's accessibility requirements, and state-specific laws is essential for building consumer trust.

    o   **Federal Trade Commission (FTC) Advertising Standards**: The FTC enforces strict advertising guidelines, requiring truthful and transparent marketing practices.

    o   **Americans with Disabilities Act (ADA)**: Online platforms and services must comply with ADA standards to ensure accessibility for users with disabilities.

    o   **State-Level Consumer Protection Laws**: Some states, like California, have additional regulations on data privacy (CCPA) and environmental standards, requiring businesses to stay informed on regional requirements.

2. **UK: Consumer Rights and Data Protection Laws**
    The UK's consumer protection and data privacy laws are robust, with the Data Protection Act and Consumer Rights Act setting high standards for online businesses. Ensuring compliance with these laws is essential for protecting customer data and delivering fair, transparent services.

    o   **Data Protection Act (DPA)**: The DPA, in alignment with GDPR, mandates that businesses protect customer data and process it responsibly.

    o   **Consumer Rights Act**: The Consumer Rights Act ensures that products are of satisfactory quality, fit for purpose, and as described, providing customers with recourse if these standards are not met.

- o **Fair Trading and Advertising Standards**: The Advertising Standards Authority (ASA) enforces rules around advertising transparency, prohibiting misleading claims and ensuring fair marketing practices.

3. **Europe: Harmonised Standards and Country-Specific Regulations**

   The EU offers a harmonised regulatory environment for cross-border trade, but individual countries may have additional requirements. Compliance with both EU and national regulations is essential for businesses looking to operate across Europe.

   - o **General Data Protection Regulation (GDPR)**: GDPR compliance is mandatory for handling customer data across the EU, requiring clear consent and strict data protection measures.

   - o **Cross-Border E-commerce Compliance**: EU laws facilitate cross-border e-commerce, but businesses must be aware of VAT, import/export rules, and product labelling requirements.

   - o **National Standards and Consumer Protection**: While EU regulations provide a framework, countries like Germany and France have additional consumer protection standards, particularly around product safety and advertising.

Conclusion

Navigating the global digital economy requires a nuanced understanding of cultural, economic, and regulatory differences. For businesses, success in international markets involves more than simply translating a website or accepting multiple currencies; it requires a commitment to understanding local values, adapting pricing and product offerings, and ensuring regulatory compliance.

Adapting to cultural and economic differences allows businesses to connect meaningfully with customers in each region, fostering trust, loyalty, and a positive brand image. By respecting local preferences and aligning with economic realities, companies can expand their reach and thrive in the diverse landscape of the digital economy. As we move to the next chapter, we will explore specific digital opportunities, including e-commerce, content creation, and blockchain, equipping readers with actionable insights to succeed globally.

3. The Skills Needed for Digital Success

In the digital economy, success requires a mix of technical expertise, adaptable soft skills, and a proactive approach to learning and innovation. While technical skills are essential for navigating digital tools and platforms, soft skills like communication, adaptability, and critical thinking are equally vital for teamwork and problem-solving. This section outlines the critical skills required for digital success, the mindset needed to adapt to change, and the learning resources that make it possible to acquire and develop these skills across the USA, UK, Europe, and beyond.

3.1 Technical Skills vs. Soft Skills

The digital economy demands a range of skills, with technical abilities often taking centre stage. However, soft skills are equally important, enabling individuals to communicate, collaborate, and solve problems effectively. This balance between technical and soft skills is essential for building resilient, innovative teams and thriving in the fast-paced digital landscape.

3.1.1 Essential Technical Skills for the Digital Economy

Technical skills form the backbone of the digital economy, enabling individuals to work with digital tools, manage data, and develop solutions that drive innovation. Here, we explore the most sought-after technical skills across different regions and industries.

1. **Data Analysis and Interpretation**
   As data becomes central to business decision-making, the ability to interpret and analyse data is increasingly valuable. Data analysis skills allow individuals to make data-driven decisions, optimise processes, and uncover insights that support strategic planning.

- o **USA: Demand for Data Scientists**
  In the USA, data science is a high-demand field, with sectors like technology, healthcare, and finance seeking skilled data analysts and scientists. Many American companies offer specific training programs in data analysis, making it a priority skill across industries.

- o **UK: Data Skills in Public and Private Sectors**
  The UK government and private sectors alike value data skills, with particular emphasis on using data for decision-making in fields like finance, retail, and public health.

- o **Europe: GDPR-Compliant Data Management**
  In Europe, data analysis skills are crucial, but they must align with GDPR regulations. Knowledge of data privacy laws is essential for European data analysts, who work across industries like e-commerce, finance, and technology.

2. **Digital Marketing and SEO**
   Digital marketing, including search engine optimisation (SEO), is essential for building brand presence online. Skills in this area enable professionals to attract, engage, and retain customers through strategic online content and advertising.

   - o **USA: Digital Marketing Innovation**
     In the USA, digital marketing skills are critical, with professionals using data-driven strategies to improve customer engagement. American marketers are also early adopters of SEO and social media marketing techniques.

   - o **UK: Focus on Content Marketing and SEO**
     UK businesses emphasise SEO and content marketing, with a focus on building strong, localised digital presences. SEO professionals

and content creators are in high demand in sectors such as retail, tourism, and education.

- o **Europe: Multi-Language Marketing and Compliance**
  In Europe, digital marketers often need multilingual skills and knowledge of local regulations. SEO and digital marketing strategies must be tailored to diverse markets, with sensitivity to cultural and linguistic differences.

3. **Cybersecurity and IT Skills**
   With the increase in digital activity comes the need for robust cybersecurity measures. Cybersecurity skills are essential to protect sensitive information, maintain consumer trust, and prevent cyber threats.

   - o **USA: Advanced Cybersecurity Initiatives**
     In the USA, cybersecurity is a top priority, especially in industries such as finance, healthcare, and government. Many companies seek skilled cybersecurity professionals to guard against data breaches and cyber attacks.

   - o **UK: Focus on Cybersecurity in Financial Services**
     Cybersecurity is crucial in the UK's financial services sector, with a growing demand for cybersecurity experts who can protect against data theft and comply with strict data protection regulations.

   - o **Europe: Compliance with Data Security Standards**
     Europe's emphasis on data protection, guided by GDPR, makes cybersecurity a highly valued skill. European cybersecurity professionals work in diverse fields, from banking to government services, where data security is critical.

3.1.2 Critical Soft Skills for Digital Success

While technical skills are important, soft skills enable individuals to collaborate effectively, adapt to changing environments, and think critically. Soft skills complement technical expertise, making them indispensable in the digital economy.

1. **Adaptability and Flexibility**
   The digital economy is dynamic, requiring individuals who can adjust to new tools, technologies, and workflows. Adaptability ensures resilience in a rapidly changing environment, enabling professionals to embrace innovation and pivot as needed.

   o **USA: Emphasis on Innovation**
      American companies value adaptability, especially in fast-evolving fields like technology and digital marketing. The ability to learn quickly and stay up-to-date with industry trends is highly regarded.

   o **UK: Flexible Work Environments**
      With the UK's shift to hybrid and remote work, adaptability is a sought-after skill. Professionals who can adjust to flexible work arrangements and digital tools are valuable in diverse industries.

   o **Europe: Adaptability Across Cultural Contexts**
      In Europe, adaptability often involves working across different languages and cultural contexts. European professionals must be flexible in their approach to accommodate regional variations and regulatory differences.

2. **Communication and Collaboration**
   Effective communication is essential for working in cross-functional teams, especially in a digital economy where remote work and digital tools are common. Strong

communication skills enable professionals to convey ideas clearly and collaborate across departments.

- o **USA: Digital Communication Skills**
  In the USA, digital communication is integral to remote and hybrid work environments. Professionals with experience in digital collaboration tools, such as Slack and Zoom, are highly valued.

- o **UK: Emphasis on Clear, Concise Communication**
  UK employers prioritise professionals who can communicate clearly and concisely, both in person and through digital channels, to ensure efficient collaboration.

- o **Europe: Multilingual Communication Abilities**
  European companies value multilingualism, especially in roles that involve client interactions or international teamwork. Professionals who can communicate in multiple languages are highly regarded.

3. **Critical Thinking and Problem-Solving**
   The digital economy requires professionals who can assess information, analyse data, and solve complex problems. Critical thinking skills help individuals navigate challenges, make informed decisions, and drive business success.

- o **USA: Data-Driven Problem-Solving**
  American businesses place a high value on data-driven decision-making, so critical thinking skills are often linked to data analysis and strategic planning.

- o **UK: Analytical Skills in Key Sectors**
  In the UK, critical thinking is essential in sectors such as finance, healthcare, and technology,

where professionals must assess risks and devise effective solutions.

- ○ **Europe: Strategic Decision-Making Across Diverse Markets**
  European companies often operate in diverse markets, requiring strategic thinking and problem-solving skills that account for regional variations in consumer behaviour and regulations.

3.1.3 Blending Technical and Soft Skills for Digital Success

Combining technical skills with strong soft skills is essential for building a successful career in the digital economy. This balance enables professionals to leverage digital tools effectively while communicating, adapting, and collaborating in a dynamic environment.

1. **USA: Cross-Functional Skills for Versatile Professionals**
   American companies value cross-functional skills that enable professionals to work across departments, from IT and marketing to data analytics and customer service.

   - ○ **Interdisciplinary Roles**: Many companies in the USA create interdisciplinary roles that require both technical expertise and communication skills, such as data storytelling or UX design.

   - ○ **Team-Oriented Work Culture**: Collaboration is integral to American business culture, with cross-functional skills ensuring professionals can contribute to diverse teams.

   - ○ **Upskilling for Versatility**: Many professionals invest in additional certifications to blend technical and soft skills, enhancing their versatility in the workplace.

2. **UK: Skills for Collaborative, Innovative Teams**

   The UK's emphasis on collaboration and innovation has led to a demand for professionals with well-rounded skill sets that include technical proficiency and effective interpersonal skills.

   o **Integrated Skill Development**: Many UK employers support integrated skill development, where employees can attend workshops that cover both technical and soft skills.

   o **Value on Interpersonal Communication**: British companies value professionals who can communicate effectively, especially in client-facing roles or project-based teams.

   o **Innovation Through Diverse Skill Sets**: The UK's startup culture prioritises professionals who bring diverse skills to the table, fostering innovation and adaptability.

3. **Europe: Combining Skills for Multinational Operations**

   European companies often require professionals who can adapt to multilingual, multicultural environments. Blending technical and soft skills is essential for navigating the complexities of Europe's diverse markets.

   o **Bilingual or Multilingual Expertise**: Many European roles require language skills alongside technical abilities, particularly in sectors like marketing and customer service.

   o **Adaptability to Local Markets**: Professionals are expected to adapt both their technical and interpersonal approaches based on regional needs and preferences.

   o **Focus on Continuous Learning**: Europe's emphasis on lifelong learning encourages professionals to continually build both technical and soft skills to meet evolving industry demands.

3.2 Building a Digital-Ready Mindset

The digital economy isn't just about the skills one possesses—it's about the mindset that drives adaptation, innovation, and resilience. A digital-ready mindset allows professionals to stay current with technological advancements, embrace change, and continuously improve. This section outlines the qualities and habits that comprise a digital-ready mindset, highlighting strategies for building this adaptable approach to work and learning.

3.2.1 Embracing Change and Continuous Learning

A core component of a digital-ready mindset is the ability to embrace change and commit to continuous learning. The rapid pace of digital transformation means that professionals need to keep updating their skills and knowledge to remain relevant and effective in their roles.

1. **USA: Lifelong Learning in a Fast-Paced Economy**
   In the USA, where digital transformation is fast-paced, professionals are expected to stay informed about new developments in their fields. The culture of lifelong learning is supported by numerous resources and programmes that promote skill-building and adaptation.

   o **Emphasis on Professional Development**: Many American companies offer in-house training programmes to help employees stay up-to-date with industry trends and technologies.

   o **Adapting to Technological Change**: A digital-ready mindset in the USA includes a proactive approach to learning new tools and software, with an emphasis on agility.

o **Frequent Skills Assessment**: American professionals often assess their skills annually, identifying gaps and seeking learning opportunities to stay competitive.

2. **UK: Focus on Career Longevity and Skill Diversification**

   In the UK, continuous learning is viewed as essential for career longevity, particularly as digital roles evolve. Many British professionals focus on skill diversification, equipping themselves with a broad set of skills to adapt to changes in the job market.

   o **Support for Upskilling and Reskilling**: The UK government supports lifelong learning initiatives, including apprenticeships and upskilling programmes for those looking to shift careers.

   o **Adaptability in Digital Roles**: British employers value employees who are willing to adapt to digital tools and processes, especially in industries like finance and healthcare.

   o **Skill Diversification**: UK professionals often pursue certifications or training in complementary skills, making them more versatile and prepared for changes in their fields.

3. **Europe: Emphasis on Lifelong Learning and Education Access**
   Europe has a strong tradition of lifelong learning, supported by accessible education and training opportunities. Many European countries encourage a culture of continuous improvement, with a focus on upskilling as a pathway to career advancement.

   o **Government-Funded Learning Initiatives**: European governments frequently subsidise educational programmes, including digital skills training, making continuous learning accessible for all.

   o **Focus on Formal Education and Short Courses**: Europeans often balance formal education with short courses that address specific digital skills, enabling them to remain adaptable in dynamic industries.

   o **Cultural Emphasis on Self-Improvement**: In Europe, continuous learning is culturally valued, with professionals prioritising self-improvement through online courses, workshops, and training events.

3.2.2 Developing Resilience and Problem-Solving Abilities

Digital work environments present unique challenges, from technical issues to rapidly changing software tools. Building resilience and developing problem-solving abilities are essential for navigating these challenges and staying productive in the digital economy.

1. **USA: Resilience in Competitive Workplaces**
   In the USA, the competitive nature of many industries demands resilience. Professionals are encouraged to handle setbacks constructively and find solutions to problems as they arise, particularly in fast-paced sectors like technology and finance.

- o **Encouragement of Innovation and Experimentation**: American workplaces often support experimentation, allowing employees to learn from mistakes and build resilience through trial and error.

- o **Stress Management Resources**: Many US companies offer wellness programmes that include stress management tools, helping employees maintain resilience in high-pressure roles.

- o **Focus on Solution-Oriented Thinking**: In the USA, solution-oriented thinking is a valued skill, with employees encouraged to identify issues and develop actionable solutions independently.

2. **UK: Cultivating Resilience in Flexible Work Environments**
   The UK's shift towards remote and hybrid work has led to an emphasis on resilience, as professionals navigate the challenges of adapting to new work environments and digital tools.

   - o **Support for Mental Health and Wellbeing**: Many UK companies provide mental health resources, recognising that resilience is strengthened through well-being support.

   - o **Flexible Problem-Solving**: UK professionals are encouraged to think flexibly and adopt creative approaches to problem-solving, particularly in project-based and collaborative roles.

   - o **Building Independence in Remote Work**: With the rise of remote work, UK professionals are often expected to solve problems independently, developing resilience as they adapt to self-directed work.

3. **Europe: Resilience Through Collaborative Work**
   European workplaces often foster resilience through collaboration and teamwork. Professionals are encouraged to seek support from colleagues, making resilience a collective effort that strengthens problem-solving abilities across teams.

   o **Collaboration and Shared Problem-Solving**: In Europe, resilience is often developed through collaborative problem-solving, where teams work together to address challenges.

   o **Work-Life Balance for Resilience**: Many European countries emphasise work-life balance, helping professionals maintain resilience by managing stress and avoiding burnout.

   o **Supportive Work Environments**: European companies often create supportive environments that encourage open communication, allowing employees to seek assistance and guidance when facing challenges.

3.2.3 Fostering a Growth Mindset for Long-Term Success

A growth mindset—the belief that skills and abilities can be developed through hard work and dedication—is essential for thriving in the digital economy. Professionals with a growth mindset view challenges as learning opportunities, enabling them to adapt and excel in new environments.

1. **USA: Growth Mindset in Innovation-Driven Industries**
   The USA, known for its culture of innovation, promotes a growth mindset as a way to encourage creativity, perseverance, and success. This mindset is especially important in fields like technology, where constant evolution requires continuous improvement.

- o **Encouragement of Goal Setting**: Many American companies encourage employees to set personal and professional goals, fostering a growth mindset by rewarding progress and improvement.

- o **Opportunities for Skill Development**: American workplaces often offer opportunities for skill development and mentorship, helping employees view challenges as chances to learn.

- o **Recognition of Achievements**: By recognising both small and large achievements, US companies reinforce the value of persistence and self-improvement in career growth.

2. **UK: Growth Mindset for Career Progression**
In the UK, professionals with a growth mindset are often more successful in advancing their careers, particularly in sectors like finance, law, and healthcare, where continuous learning is valued.

- o **Promotion of Career Development Plans**: UK employers often support career development plans that include mentorship, training, and goal-setting, fostering a growth mindset in the workforce.

- o **Cultural Focus on Self-Improvement**: The UK's emphasis on professional development encourages a growth mindset, with many professionals viewing skill-building as essential to career longevity.

- o **Learning from Feedback**: UK companies value feedback, helping employees learn from constructive criticism and apply it to future projects.

3. **Europe: Growth Mindset for Cross-Cultural Adaptability**
A growth mindset is crucial in Europe, where

professionals often work in multicultural environments. Adapting to different cultures and languages requires a willingness to learn and grow, making this mindset essential.

- o **Learning from Diverse Perspectives**: European workplaces often bring together professionals from different backgrounds, fostering a growth mindset through exposure to diverse ideas.

- o **Language and Cultural Adaptability**: Many European professionals embrace the challenge of learning new languages or adapting to different cultural norms, reinforcing their growth mindset.

- o **Focus on Lifelong Improvement**: The European emphasis on lifelong learning and personal development aligns well with the growth mindset, promoting continuous improvement across all career stages.

Conclusion

In the digital economy, a digital-ready mindset is as important as any technical skill. Professionals who embrace change, build resilience, and maintain a growth mindset are better equipped to handle the challenges and opportunities of a rapidly evolving workplace. With continuous learning, adaptability, and a positive approach to self-improvement, individuals can navigate the complexities of the digital landscape and thrive in their careers.

By understanding and fostering these qualities, individuals in the USA, UK, and Europe can position themselves for success in any digital role. As we move forward, we will explore the platforms and resources available to help professionals acquire and develop the skills they need, setting them on a path toward long-term success in the digital economy.

3.3 Learning Resources and Platforms

In the digital economy, learning has never been more accessible. Online platforms, virtual classes, and a wealth of digital resources offer professionals the opportunity to build relevant skills on their own schedule and often at an affordable cost. This section explores the primary resources and platforms that support skill development for digital success, covering formal educational institutions, online learning platforms, and experiential learning opportunities.

3.3.1 Formal Education and Certification Programmes

Formal education and certification programmes provide structured, credible paths for learning. From university degrees to industry-specific certifications, these options are valuable for building foundational knowledge and gaining recognised credentials in digital skills.

1. **USA: Emphasis on Industry Certifications and Microcredentials**

   In the USA, industry certifications and microcredentials are highly valued, particularly in fields like IT, digital marketing, and data science. Many professionals pursue certifications to validate their skills and enhance their employability.

   o **Tech Certifications from Recognised Organisations**: Certifications from organisations like CompTIA, Cisco, and Microsoft are highly regarded in the USA, helping professionals in IT and network administration build their credibility.

   o **University-Led Microcredentials**: Many American universities, including MIT and Stanford, offer microcredential programmes in data science, digital marketing, and cybersecurity. These short courses provide focused, industry-relevant training.

- o **Professional Development Funding**: Many US employers fund certification courses for their employees, recognising that formal credentials can add value to their workforce.

2. **UK: Government-Backed Apprenticeships and Professional Certifications**
   In the UK, professional certifications and government-backed apprenticeships are popular pathways for building skills in fields like finance, healthcare, and digital technology. These programmes provide a blend of formal education and hands-on experience.

   - o **Apprenticeship Programmes**: Government-backed apprenticeships provide hands-on training in digital skills, particularly in fields like software development, cybersecurity, and digital marketing.

   - o **Chartered Certifications**: Certifications from organisations like the Chartered Institute of Marketing (CIM) and Chartered Institute for IT (BCS) are highly regarded in the UK, providing credible qualifications for professionals.

   - o **Universities Offering Short Courses**: Many UK universities, such as the University of Oxford and London School of Economics, offer online short courses in digital skills, allowing professionals to learn flexibly.

3. **Europe: Access to Subsidised Learning and Certifications**

   European professionals benefit from access to subsidised education and certification programmes, with many governments supporting lifelong learning initiatives. Certification programmes are popular for building skills in engineering, IT, and digital marketing.

   o **Government-Subsidised Training**: In countries like Germany and France, government-subsidised training programmes provide affordable access to certifications in high-demand skills, such as data science and software engineering.

   o **Professional Certificates and Diplomas**: Certifications from recognised organisations like TÜV (Germany) and IAB Europe (digital marketing) validate skills and enhance employability in digital fields.

   o **European Universities and Technical Colleges**: Many European universities offer specialised courses in digital skills, including coding bootcamps and diploma programmes that align with industry needs.

3.3.2 Online Learning Platforms and Self-Paced Courses

Online learning platforms have transformed education, offering flexibility and a wide range of courses that make skill development accessible to all. These platforms provide options for self-paced learning, allowing individuals to develop digital skills at their own speed and convenience.

1. **USA: Leading Online Platforms for Digital Skills**
   In the USA, online learning platforms like Coursera, Udacity, and LinkedIn Learning are widely used for professional development. These platforms offer courses

in popular areas like data science, digital marketing, and business management.

- o **Coursera and Udacity**: Known for tech-focused courses, these platforms partner with leading universities and companies to offer certificates in AI, machine learning, and software development.

- o **LinkedIn Learning for Professional Skills**: LinkedIn Learning provides self-paced courses in business, creative, and technical skills, with popular modules on leadership, project management, and digital tools.

- o **Skillshare for Creative Professionals**: Skillshare is popular among American creatives, offering courses in design, video production, and illustration, ideal for freelancers in digital media.

2. **UK: Focus on Accessible Online Education**
   In the UK, platforms like FutureLearn and Open University provide accessible online courses that cater to both beginners and advanced learners, covering a range of digital skills, including coding, digital marketing, and data analytics.

   - o **FutureLearn Partnerships**: FutureLearn partners with UK universities to offer accredited courses in data science, coding, and business strategy, catering to professionals seeking flexible learning.

   - o **Open University Digital Courses**: Open University's online courses include modules on digital literacy, data analytics, and information technology, providing high-quality education that fits busy schedules.

   - o **Learn Direct for Vocational Training**: Learn Direct offers vocational training for adults, with courses in areas like IT and business administration, supporting those looking to upskill or reskill.

3. **Europe: Multi-Language Online Learning Options**
   European professionals benefit from online learning platforms that offer multi-language options and culturally relevant content. Platforms like EdX, 42, and Iversity provide digital skills training with regional adaptations.

   o **EdX Courses with European Universities**: EdX offers digital skills courses in partnership with European universities, including coding, AI, and digital strategy programmes.

   o **42 for Coding and IT Skills**: The French-founded 42 provides coding bootcamps that are free to participants, with campuses across Europe, offering hands-on coding and software development training.

   o **Iversity for Professional Development**: Iversity provides online courses in digital marketing, project management, and entrepreneurship, tailored to European markets and available in multiple languages.

3.3.3 Experiential Learning and Practical Skill Development

Experiential learning, including internships, freelancing, and project-based work, allows individuals to gain hands-on experience in real-world settings. These opportunities enable professionals to apply digital skills in practice, reinforcing their learning and building confidence.

1. **USA: Internships and Freelance Work for Hands-On Experience**
   In the USA, internships and freelance work are common ways for professionals to build experience. Many professionals start with internships to gain exposure, and then transition to freelancing for greater flexibility.

   o **Internships in Digital Sectors**: American companies in tech, marketing, and finance offer internships that provide practical experience in digital roles, from coding to data analysis.

   o **Freelancing on Platforms like Upwork and Fiverr**: Many Americans build digital portfolios through freelancing, working on platforms like Upwork and Fiverr to gain experience in digital marketing, graphic design, and software development.

   o **Project-Based Learning in Bootcamps**: Coding bootcamps and tech training programmes in the USA often include project-based learning, allowing students to create real-world projects to showcase their skills.

2. **UK: Industry Placements and Work-Based Learning**
   In the UK, industry placements and work-based learning are integral to building practical skills. Programmes that combine study with work experience are popular, particularly in fields like IT and engineering.

   o **Placement Years in University Courses**: Many UK universities offer "sandwich" courses, which include a year-long industry placement to provide practical experience in digital roles.

   o **Apprenticeships in Digital Fields**: Digital apprenticeships combine classroom learning with hands-on work, allowing participants to gain valuable experience in areas like cybersecurity, web development, and digital marketing.

- **Freelance Networks and Portfolios**: UK freelancers often build portfolios by working on platforms like PeoplePerHour, gaining experience in digital media, IT, and consulting.

3. **Europe: Vocational Training and Dual Education Systems**

   European countries have strong traditions of vocational training and dual education systems, combining classroom instruction with practical work experience. This model is particularly effective in preparing professionals for digital roles.

   - **Dual Education Systems in Germany and Austria**: In Germany and Austria, the dual education system provides hands-on training in fields like IT, software engineering, and digital media, preparing students for industry-specific roles.

   - **EU Internships and Traineeships**: European students often gain practical experience through EU-funded internships and traineeships, working in digital roles in government, NGOs, and private companies.

   - **Freelance Opportunities on Regional Platforms**: Many Europeans use local freelancing platforms like Malt (France) or Workana (Spain), building experience in digital roles like UX design, copywriting, and data analysis.

Conclusion

Success in the digital economy depends on continuous learning and skill development, facilitated by a wealth of educational resources and platforms. From formal education and certifications to online courses and experiential learning, professionals have access to diverse pathways for building digital skills. By leveraging these resources, individuals in the USA, UK, and Europe can stay competitive, up-to-date, and prepared for a future driven by digital transformation.

In the next chapter, we will delve into specific opportunities within the digital economy, such as e-commerce, content creation, and blockchain, providing actionable insights for those looking to expand their digital presence and generate sustainable income streams.

Chapter 2: Making Money Online – Blogging, YouTube, and Social Media

The internet offers countless opportunities to make money online, with blogging, YouTube, and social media being some of the most accessible platforms. This chapter provides a step-by-step guide on how to leverage these platforms for income generation. Whether you're looking to turn a hobby into a source of profit or build a full-time online business, understanding the mechanics of each platform is essential. We'll start with blogging, covering the fundamentals of creating valuable content, monetising a blog, and attracting a loyal readership.

2.1 Blogging for Profit

Blogging can be a powerful way to generate income, establish authority in a particular field, and build a loyal audience. However, profitable blogging requires careful planning, from selecting a niche and creating engaging content to understanding the most effective monetisation methods and building organic traffic. This section explores each of these essential steps, providing a comprehensive framework to start making money through blogging.

2.1.1 Niche Selection and Content Creation

Choosing the right niche and creating valuable content are the foundations of a profitable blog. A well-defined niche helps attract a targeted audience, while high-quality content establishes trust and keeps readers returning. Here's how to approach niche selection and create content that resonates with your audience.

1. **Identifying a Profitable Niche**
   Selecting a niche involves balancing your interests with market demand. A profitable niche should align with your passions, skills, and knowledge while also

appealing to a specific audience with a need or problem that your content can solve.

- **Researching Market Demand**: Tools like Google Trends, Ahrefs, and SEMrush can help you analyse search volume and competition in various niches. Look for topics that have consistent interest but aren't oversaturated, ensuring you can establish a presence without competing against top brands.

- **Audience Analysis**: Understanding your audience is crucial. In the USA, niches around health, finance, and lifestyle are popular, while the UK audience often engages with sustainability, tech, and fashion blogs. European audiences may have specific preferences based on regional interests, such as local travel or language-specific content.

- **Balancing Passion and Profit**: Choose a niche that excites you; blogging requires consistency and dedication. A profitable blog often takes time to establish, so having genuine interest in your chosen topic will help you maintain momentum.

2. **Creating Engaging and Valuable Content**
Quality content is essential to building trust with your audience and encouraging repeat visits. Your content should be informative, engaging, and actionable, providing real value to readers.

- **Content Structure and Readability**: Organise posts with clear headings, short paragraphs, and bullet points for readability. This approach caters to readers who skim articles and aligns with SEO best practices, especially for attracting traffic in English-speaking markets like the USA and UK.

- o **Visuals and Multimedia**: Visual content, such as images, infographics, and videos, enhances engagement. Studies show that readers spend more time on posts with multimedia elements, which is particularly effective in visual-driven niches like travel and fashion.

- o **Consistency and Posting Schedule**: A regular posting schedule helps retain readers and signals to search engines that your blog is active. Weekly or bi-weekly posts are ideal for keeping readers engaged without overwhelming them.

3. **Building Authority and Expertise**

   Readers are more likely to trust and follow blogs that demonstrate expertise. Establishing authority in your niche helps attract loyal followers and can lead to higher engagement and monetisation opportunities.

   - o **In-Depth, Informative Posts**: Long-form content that thoroughly addresses readers' questions or problems establishes your blog as a trusted resource. Detailed posts also perform well on search engines, improving visibility.

   - o **Guest Posting and Collaboration**: Building connections with other bloggers and industry experts can help broaden your reach. Guest posts on reputable sites allow you to showcase expertise, link back to your blog, and increase your audience.

   - o **Regularly Updating Content**: Keeping your content updated is important for maintaining authority, especially in fast-changing niches like technology or finance. Updating old posts with new insights helps retain relevance and improve SEO rankings.

2.1.2 Monetising Through Ads and Affiliate Marketing

Monetisation is a crucial step in turning a blog into a source of income. Ads and affiliate marketing are two of the most common revenue streams for bloggers. This section provides strategies for setting up ads, choosing affiliate programmes, and maximising earning potential.

1. **Setting Up Ad Revenue Streams**
   Ads are a simple way to start monetising a blog, with options ranging from display ads to sponsored content. Each ad type has different revenue potential and requirements, so choosing the right one depends on your niche, audience size, and blog content.

   o **Google AdSense and Ad Networks**: Google AdSense is a popular option for new bloggers, offering a straightforward way to earn through pay-per-click ads. As your traffic grows, joining premium ad networks like Mediavine or AdThrive can increase earnings, especially for blogs with significant traffic from the USA, UK, and Europe.

   o **Sponsored Posts and Banner Ads**: Many brands pay for sponsored posts or banner ads on blogs with relevant audiences. Reach out to companies in your niche, or join networks that connect bloggers with advertisers, to create mutually beneficial sponsorship opportunities.

   o **Managing Ad Placement for User Experience**: Ads can be intrusive if not managed carefully. Placing ads strategically—such as in sidebars or between sections—maintains a balance between monetisation and user experience, encouraging readers to stay engaged with your content.

2. **Affiliate Marketing: Choosing and Promoting Products**
   Affiliate marketing allows bloggers to earn a commission by promoting products or services through affiliate links. This monetisation method is particularly

effective for niche blogs that can offer targeted recommendations.

- o **Selecting Affiliate Programmes**: Amazon Associates, ShareASale, and CJ Affiliate are popular affiliate networks that provide access to various brands. Choose programmes that align with your blog's niche to ensure recommendations are relevant and credible.

- o **Creating Product-Focused Content**: Reviews, product comparisons, and "best of" lists are effective for affiliate marketing. These types of posts attract readers with high purchase intent, increasing the likelihood of conversions.

- o **Transparent Disclosure of Affiliate Links**: Transparency is key to maintaining reader trust. Include disclosures in posts to inform readers about affiliate links, as this honesty fosters trust and complies with legal requirements in the USA, UK, and EU.

3. **Maximising Earnings with Optimised Placement**
   Strategic placement of ads and affiliate links within your content can boost click-through rates and increase earnings. Experiment with placements to see which positions generate the best results without disrupting the reading experience.

- o **In-Content Links and Call-to-Actions**: Placing affiliate links within content, especially after mentioning a product's benefits, is more effective than isolating links at the end of a post.

- o **Sidebar and Footer Links**: For blogs with high traffic, placing affiliate links in sidebars or footers can provide passive revenue without being overly intrusive.

- o **Testing Link Performance**: Tools like Google Analytics and affiliate dashboards allow you to monitor click-through rates, helping you refine placement strategies for optimal performance.

2.1.3 SEO and Traffic Growth Strategies (Continued)

Generating traffic is the lifeline of a successful blog, directly impacting ad revenue, affiliate sales, and overall visibility. With search engine optimisation (SEO) at the core, implementing effective traffic growth strategies can elevate a blog from obscurity to prominence, bringing in consistent and engaged readership.

---

1. **Keyword Research and Optimisation (Continued)**
   Effective keyword research lays the groundwork for SEO success. With the right keywords, bloggers can attract readers who are specifically interested in their niche, increasing the potential for engagement and conversion.

   o **Long-Tail Keyword Focus**: Long-tail keywords, which are more specific (e.g., "vegan meal prep recipes for beginners" rather than "vegan recipes"), often have lower competition and higher conversion rates. This approach is particularly beneficial for new blogs in the USA, UK, and Europe, as it allows them to target niche audiences.

   o **Internal Linking for SEO**: Internal linking is a technique that connects one page of a blog to another, helping to improve SEO by guiding readers through related content. This also reduces bounce rates and keeps readers on the site longer.

   o **Optimising for Mobile and Page Speed**: Mobile-friendliness and fast page loading times are crucial for SEO, as search engines prioritise user experience. Blogs should ensure that their design is responsive and loads quickly on all devices, especially given the high mobile usage rates in markets like the UK and Europe.

2. **Building Backlinks and Authority (Continued)**
High-quality backlinks are a cornerstone of SEO, as they signal to search engines that your content is credible and authoritative. Building backlinks can take time but is essential for long-term SEO success.

  o **Directory Listings and Niche Sites**: Listing your blog on reputable directories and niche websites can provide valuable backlinks. Directories focused on specific interests (e.g., health, travel) help attract targeted traffic, increasing the likelihood of relevant backlinks.

  o **Creating Linkable Assets**: Content that other bloggers and websites want to link to—such as original research, tutorials, or case studies—acts as a "linkable asset." For example, a comprehensive "guide to sustainable fashion in Europe" could attract backlinks from eco-conscious fashion sites.

  o **Leveraging Content Round-Ups and Collaborations**: Reaching out to bloggers who create weekly or monthly round-ups can provide link-building opportunities. Collaborations on content, like joint guides or interviews, also generate organic backlinks while strengthening network ties.

3. **Social Media and Community Engagement (Continued)**
Social media platforms play a significant role in driving blog traffic, providing a space to share content, interact with readers, and build a community around your brand. Each platform has unique strengths that can be leveraged based on your audience.

o **Choosing the Right Platforms**: Identifying the platforms that align with your niche is critical. For instance, Pinterest is highly effective for lifestyle and DIY blogs, while Twitter may be more useful for finance or tech-related content.

o **Engaging with Followers and Other Bloggers**: Social media is not just for promotion but also for building connections. Engaging with followers and other bloggers by commenting on posts, joining groups, or sharing others' content fosters a sense of community.

o **Content Repurposing for Broader Reach**: Repurposing blog content into various formats (e.g., infographics, short videos, or slides) enables broader reach across different social platforms. A "top travel tips" blog post could be transformed into a Pinterest infographic, Instagram carousel, or Twitter thread to attract varied audiences.

Conclusion

Building a profitable blog requires a multi-faceted approach, from choosing the right niche and creating valuable content to implementing effective monetisation and SEO strategies. By carefully selecting a niche, focusing on quality content, and utilising both advertising and affiliate marketing, bloggers can create revenue streams that grow with their audience. SEO and social media strategies further enhance a blog's visibility, driving consistent traffic that leads to higher earning potential.

As we move into the next section of this chapter, we will explore additional avenues for online income, focusing on YouTube and social media as profitable platforms. With actionable strategies and real-world examples, these insights will guide readers in building and monetising a digital presence that goes beyond traditional blogging.

2.2 YouTube for Profit

YouTube has become a powerful platform for income generation, offering creators various monetisation options from ad revenue and sponsorships to affiliate marketing and merchandise. However, building a successful YouTube channel requires planning, consistency, and a deep understanding of audience interests. This section will cover the essential steps to creating, growing, and monetising a profitable YouTube channel, with insights on how to adapt strategies for markets like the USA, UK, and Europe.

2.2.1 Finding a Niche and Creating Engaging Content

As with blogging, finding a profitable niche and creating engaging content are critical for YouTube success. The right niche helps you attract a specific audience, while compelling content keeps viewers coming back for more.

1. **Identifying a Profitable YouTube Niche**
   A well-defined niche allows creators to stand out in a competitive space and build a loyal following. Identifying a niche involves evaluating personal interests, audience demand, and revenue potential.

   o **Researching Trending Niches**: Tools like YouTube Trends, Google Trends, and TubeBuddy help identify niches with rising popularity. Popular niches include tech reviews, health and fitness, and lifestyle vlogs, each appealing to specific audiences in the USA, UK, and Europe.

   o **Balancing Passion and Profitability**: Selecting a niche that excites you is essential, as maintaining a consistent upload schedule can be challenging without genuine interest. Look for topics that offer a balance between profitability and personal enthusiasm.

- o **Analysing Competitors**: Researching successful YouTube channels in your chosen niche can provide insights into what works. Pay attention to content themes, video style, and engagement levels to identify what attracts viewers.

2. **Planning and Producing High-Quality Videos**
Quality content is key to growing a YouTube channel. Videos that are visually appealing, well-edited, and informative tend to perform better and attract repeat viewers.

- o **Investing in Essential Equipment**: While it's possible to start with basic tools, upgrading to a good-quality camera, microphone, and lighting setup can improve video quality and viewer retention. This is particularly important for channels aiming to attract a global audience.

- o **Editing and Post-Production**: Editing plays a significant role in making videos engaging. Simple editing software like iMovie and advanced tools like Adobe Premiere Pro enable creators to polish their content, add effects, and create a consistent brand style.

- o **Creating Thumbnails and Titles for Clickability**: Eye-catching thumbnails and descriptive titles are essential for attracting viewers. A/B testing different thumbnail designs and optimising titles for keywords can increase click-through rates.

3. **Building a Content Strategy and Consistent Schedule**
Consistency is crucial on YouTube, as regular uploads keep viewers engaged and signal to the platform that your channel is active. A well-planned content strategy

helps streamline production and maintain viewer interest.

- o **Setting a Content Calendar**: A content calendar helps plan video topics, filming schedules, and release dates. Aim for a balance of evergreen content (e.g., tutorials) and trending topics to attract both new and returning viewers.

- o **Batch Filming and Scheduling**: Filming multiple videos in one session (batch filming) can save time and help maintain consistency. YouTube's scheduling feature allows you to release videos on a pre-set schedule, building anticipation for new content.

- o **Engaging with Viewer Feedback**: Listening to viewer feedback and responding to comments helps create a sense of community and informs future content ideas. Understanding what resonates with your audience can shape your channel's direction.

2.2.2 Monetising a YouTube Channel

Once a channel gains traction, monetisation options on YouTube are diverse. From ad revenue to sponsorships and merchandise sales, multiple income streams allow creators to maximise their earning potential.

1. **Ad Revenue through YouTube Partner Programme**
   Joining the YouTube Partner Programme enables creators to earn revenue from ads shown on their videos. Meeting eligibility criteria, such as reaching 1,000 subscribers and 4,000 watch hours, is necessary to access this programme.

   - **Types of Ads and Earnings**: YouTube offers various ad types, including display, overlay, and skippable video ads. Earnings are influenced by factors such as ad placement, audience geography, and niche. In markets like the USA, where ad spend is higher, channels may earn more per view.

   - **Managing Ad Placements for Viewer Experience**: While more ads can increase revenue, overloading videos with ads may disrupt the viewing experience. Many creators choose to place ads strategically, such as at the start or in natural breaks.

   - **Ad Revenue Analytics**: YouTube Analytics provides insights into ad performance, enabling creators to track revenue, viewership, and engagement. Understanding which videos generate the most ad revenue can guide future content.

2. **Sponsorships and Brand Collaborations**
   Sponsored content is a lucrative income source for YouTubers, with brands paying for product placements, reviews, or dedicated videos. Collaborations are especially valuable for creators in niches with a strong commercial focus, like beauty, tech, and fitness.

- o **Approaching Brands for Sponsorships**: Once a channel gains traction, creators can approach brands in their niche or join influencer platforms like FameBit and Grapevine. Personalised pitches that demonstrate brand alignment tend to be more successful.

- o **Creating Authentic Sponsored Content**: Viewers respond best to sponsored content that feels genuine. Successful YouTubers incorporate products naturally into their videos, ensuring that promotions align with their usual content style.

- o **Setting Sponsorship Rates**: Sponsorship rates vary depending on factors like niche, audience demographics, and engagement rates. Conducting market research and negotiating fair terms are key to establishing profitable partnerships.

3. **Affiliate Marketing and Merchandise Sales**
Affiliate marketing and merchandise sales are additional revenue streams that allow creators to monetise their brand and leverage audience loyalty.

- o **Affiliate Programmes and Product Recommendations**: Many YouTubers join affiliate programmes like Amazon Associates, earning commissions for products they recommend. Product reviews, tutorials, and "favourites" videos are effective formats for promoting affiliate products.

- o **Creating Branded Merchandise**: Platforms like Teespring and Merchbar enable creators to design and sell branded merchandise. Merchandise is particularly successful for YouTubers with a loyal fan base who want to support the channel.

- o **Integrating Sales in Videos and Descriptions**: Links to affiliate products and merchandise can be included in video descriptions, cards, and end screens. Creators often add a call-to-action (CTA) encouraging viewers to check out products they've featured.

2.2.3 Growing an Audience and Building Engagement

Audience engagement is crucial for YouTube growth, as the platform prioritises videos with high watch times, likes, comments, and shares. Building a loyal following involves cultivating a community, engaging directly with viewers, and continuously improving content.

1. **Optimising for YouTube Search and Algorithm**
   YouTube's algorithm rewards videos that keep viewers engaged, so optimising videos for search and suggested content is essential for growth.

   - o **Keyword Research for YouTube**: YouTube is a search engine, so keyword optimisation plays a major role in discovery. Tools like TubeBuddy and vidIQ help creators find popular search terms relevant to their niche.

   - o **Using Tags and Descriptions Effectively**: Including keywords in video titles, descriptions, and tags improves SEO. Crafting concise but descriptive text that highlights key points and appeals to viewer interest can increase visibility.

   - o **Optimising for Viewer Retention**: YouTube values viewer retention, so keeping videos engaging from start to finish is critical. Many creators use hooks in the first 15 seconds to capture attention and encourage viewers to watch the full video.

2. **Interacting with the Community**
   Direct engagement with viewers builds community and

encourages loyalty, making viewers more likely to return for future videos. Engaging in conversations can also provide valuable feedback.

- o **Responding to Comments**: Taking the time to reply to comments helps create a personal connection with viewers. Responding to questions and thanking viewers for their feedback fosters positive engagement.

- o **Incorporating Viewer Feedback in Content**: Listening to viewers' preferences can guide content development. Many successful YouTubers actively ask their audience for suggestions, ensuring future videos resonate with viewer interests.

- o **Using Polls and Live Streams**: YouTube's community tab allows creators to engage directly with their audience through polls, posts, and live streams. These tools are effective for gathering feedback and building real-time connections.

3. **Collaborations and Cross-Promotion**
   Collaborations with other creators allow YouTubers to reach new audiences and build credibility within their niche. Cross-promotion with similar channels is a mutually beneficial way to grow viewership.

- o **Finding the Right Collaboration Partners**: Partnering with channels of a similar size or niche helps ensure a good fit. Collaborative projects like co-hosted videos or cross-promoted content can attract subscribers who share common interests.

- o **Guest Appearances and Channel Shout-Outs**: Appearing on other channels or participating in guest interviews helps increase exposure. In return, inviting guests to one's channel adds variety and draws in their audience.

- o **Promoting Across Social Media**: Cross-promoting YouTube content on other platforms like Instagram and Twitter helps drive traffic to the channel. Consistent promotion increases the likelihood of reaching a wider audience.

Conclusion

Building a profitable YouTube channel is a journey that requires careful planning, consistent content, and strategic monetisation. By selecting a niche, creating high-quality videos, and exploring diverse revenue streams, YouTubers can turn their passion into a profitable business. Success on YouTube involves both creativity and strategic growth, from optimising for the algorithm to engaging with viewers and expanding reach through collaborations.

The following section will explore the unique opportunities and strategies for monetising social media platforms like Instagram, TikTok, and Twitter. With a focus on building an authentic brand and connecting with audiences, readers will gain insights into making social media a profitable component of their online business.

2.3 Social Media for Profit

Social media has become a cornerstone of the digital economy, allowing individuals to build personal brands, engage with audiences, and create diverse revenue streams. Unlike blogging or YouTube, social media offers more interactive and immediate engagement, making it ideal for creators who enjoy connecting directly with their audience. This section covers the essential steps to building a profitable social media presence, from selecting the right platforms to establishing monetisation strategies.

2.3.1 Choosing the Right Social Media Platform

Each social media platform has its own strengths, demographics, and monetisation opportunities. Selecting the right platform is essential to reaching your target audience and establishing a profitable social media presence.

1. **Understanding Platform Strengths and Demographics**
   Different platforms attract unique audiences, and understanding these demographics helps tailor content and monetisation strategies to meet viewer expectations.

   o **Instagram's Visual Appeal**: Instagram is popular for visually engaging content, making it ideal for niches like fashion, food, travel, and lifestyle. The platform's core audience is young adults, with a strong following in the USA, UK, and Europe.

   o **TikTok's Viral Potential**: TikTok's short-form video format and powerful algorithm provide significant viral potential, especially for trends, challenges, and creative content. With a large Gen Z user base, it's effective for brands targeting younger demographics.

- o **Twitter's Focus on News and Interaction**: Twitter is ideal for real-time interaction and is popular in industries like tech, finance, and politics. The platform's emphasis on conversation allows for high engagement with audiences interested in current events.

2. **Evaluating Content Fit for Each Platform**
Content format and tone vary significantly across platforms. Choosing a platform where your content style aligns with user preferences is essential for engagement.

   - o **Visual Content on Instagram and TikTok**: High-quality images and short videos perform well on Instagram, while TikTok's algorithm rewards engaging, fast-paced videos. For creators in visually appealing niches, these platforms offer the best return on content.

   - o **Educational and Conversational Content on Twitter**: Twitter is well-suited for educational or conversational content, allowing creators to share insights, news, or engage in discussions. This platform is particularly effective for thought leadership and networking.

   - o **Utilising Multiple Platforms**: Many creators use a combination of platforms, such as Instagram and TikTok for visuals, and Twitter for engagement. Cross-posting content increases reach and helps build a cohesive online brand.

3. **Determining Monetisation Potential by Platform**
Each platform offers unique monetisation options. Understanding these options and how they align with your niche helps maximise revenue.

   - o **Instagram's Sponsored Posts and Stories**: Instagram is one of the most profitable platforms for sponsored content. Sponsored posts and stories are ideal for creators with engaged audiences in lifestyle and consumer-focused niches.

- o **TikTok's Creator Fund and Brand Partnerships**: TikTok's Creator Fund allows eligible creators to earn money based on video views, and brand partnerships on TikTok can be highly lucrative, especially for viral content.

- o **Twitter's Affiliate Marketing and Promotions**: While Twitter lacks direct monetisation features, it's effective for affiliate marketing and driving traffic to external sites, making it useful for promoting products or blog content.

2.3.2 Building an Engaged Audience

Audience engagement is key to social media success. Building a loyal following requires more than just high-quality content; it involves connecting with followers, encouraging interaction, and creating a sense of community.

1. **Creating Authentic and Valuable Content**
   Authenticity is highly valued on social media, and followers are more likely to engage with creators who share genuine insights and experiences. Content should provide value, whether through entertainment, education, or inspiration.

   - o **Storytelling for Connection**: Storytelling allows creators to build a personal connection with their audience. Sharing personal experiences, challenges, or successes fosters authenticity and encourages followers to invest in your journey.

   - o **Value-Driven Content**: Content that teaches, entertains, or inspires attracts engagement. For example, "how-to" tutorials on TikTok, aesthetic inspiration on Instagram, and thought-provoking threads on Twitter all provide tangible value to followers.

- o **Balancing Promotional and Personal Content**: While monetisation is essential, over-promotion can alienate followers. Maintain a balance between personal or value-driven content and sponsored or promotional posts to build trust.

2. **Leveraging Platform-Specific Features**
   Each social media platform has unique features designed to increase engagement. Utilising these features strategically can help boost visibility and foster interaction.

   - o **Instagram Stories, Reels, and Lives**: Instagram offers various content formats beyond regular posts. Stories provide an ephemeral, informal way to connect with followers, while Reels and Lives offer opportunities for real-time interaction and broader reach.

   - o **TikTok Challenges and Hashtags**: TikTok's hashtag challenges encourage user participation and increase visibility. Leveraging trending challenges or creating branded hashtags can boost engagement and attract new followers.

   - o **Twitter Polls and Threads**: Twitter's poll and thread features allow creators to engage in conversations with followers. Polls are effective for gauging follower interests, while threads enable in-depth discussions.

3. **Engaging Directly with Followers**
   Direct engagement strengthens community and builds loyalty. Taking time to interact with followers fosters a sense of personal connection and encourages repeat engagement.

- o **Responding to Comments and Messages**: Acknowledging comments and messages shows that you value your audience's input. Personal responses foster a more loyal and engaged following.

- o **Hosting Q&A Sessions**: Live Q&A sessions on Instagram Live or Twitter Spaces allow followers to ask questions and engage in real time, strengthening relationships and building trust.

- o **Using Community-Centric Content**: Creating community-centric content, such as follower shoutouts or highlighting user-generated content, builds a sense of inclusivity and encourages ongoing interaction.

2.3.3 Monetising Social Media Content

Once an engaged following is established, monetisation becomes viable through various methods, including sponsorships, affiliate marketing, and digital products. Each monetisation option has unique advantages and suits different types of content and audiences.

1. **Sponsored Content and Brand Collaborations**
   Sponsored posts and brand collaborations are among the most profitable options for social media creators. This form of monetisation allows creators to partner with brands that align with their niche and audience.

   - o **Finding Relevant Brand Partnerships**: Partner with brands that align with your content style and audience demographics. Many influencers connect with brands via platforms like AspireIQ and Influencity, or through direct outreach.

   - o **Creating Authentic Sponsored Posts**: Authenticity is essential for sponsored content. Rather than overly promotional posts, integrate products naturally into content to maintain trust and engagement.

- o **Negotiating Sponsorship Rates**: Rates for sponsored posts vary based on factors like audience size, engagement, and niche. Researching market rates and negotiating fair terms ensures that sponsorships are profitable and sustainable.

2. **Affiliate Marketing**
   Affiliate marketing allows creators to earn a commission by promoting products through unique links. This method is particularly effective for creators with engaged audiences interested in product recommendations.

   - o **Choosing Affiliate Programmes**: Platforms like Amazon Associates, RewardStyle, and ClickBank offer affiliate programmes across various niches. Choose programmes that fit your content and provide competitive commission rates.

   - o **Integrating Affiliate Links**: Place affiliate links strategically within content. For example, include links in Instagram Stories with swipe-up features, Twitter posts, or captions to encourage clicks.

   - o **Transparency in Affiliate Disclosures**: To maintain trust and comply with legal regulations, always disclose affiliate links clearly. Transparent communication enhances credibility and encourages followers to support your recommendations.

3. **Selling Digital Products and Services**
   Many creators diversify their income by selling digital products or services, such as e-books, online courses, or personalised consultations. This approach leverages expertise and builds additional revenue streams.

- o **E-Books and Guides**: E-books or downloadable guides are popular digital products for creators in niches like fitness, finance, and lifestyle. These products allow followers to gain in-depth knowledge and support the creator.

- o **Online Courses and Workshops**: For creators with specialised knowledge, online courses or workshops provide a valuable learning experience. Platforms like Teachable and Thinkific make it easy to host courses for followers.

- o **Consulting and Personalised Services**: Offering one-on-one consulting or personalised services, such as social media audits or fitness coaching, enables creators to provide tailored advice. This is particularly effective for creators with high expertise in a specific area.

Conclusion

Social media offers numerous paths to profitability, from brand partnerships and affiliate marketing to selling digital products. By choosing the right platform, building an engaged audience, and utilising diverse monetisation strategies, creators can turn their social media presence into a profitable venture. Success on social media requires authenticity, consistency, and a focus on audience value, ensuring long-term growth and income potential.

2.4 Building a YouTube Channel

Creating a successful YouTube channel is an exciting path to online income, with potential earnings ranging from ad revenue to sponsorships and viewer memberships. However, building a channel that attracts viewers, keeps them engaged, and turns a profit requires strategic planning. This section explores how to establish a profitable YouTube channel, from choosing the right focus to monetising effectively and fostering an engaged community of subscribers.

2.4.1 Choosing Your Channel's Focus

Selecting a focus or niche is the first step in creating a YouTube channel with clear, consistent appeal. A well-defined focus makes it easier to attract a loyal audience, plan content, and create value that resonates with viewers.

1. **Identifying a Profitable Niche**
   A profitable YouTube niche balances personal interest, market demand, and competitive advantage. Popular niches include tech reviews, lifestyle, education, and entertainment, each offering unique monetisation opportunities.

   - **Researching Audience Demand**: Tools like YouTube Trends, Google Trends, and vidIQ can reveal popular niches with rising interest. The USA, UK, and Europe each have specific audience preferences; for instance, tech reviews are popular globally, while DIY and lifestyle content may appeal more in the UK and Europe.

   - **Assessing Competition**: Analysing the competitive landscape helps identify gaps in content or unique angles. For example, in saturated niches like gaming or beauty, finding a fresh approach, such as focusing on a specific game or style, can set a channel apart.

o **Choosing a Sustainable Niche**: Maintaining a YouTube channel requires dedication and consistency. Selecting a niche that genuinely interests you ensures long-term commitment, especially in competitive spaces.

2. **Defining Your Target Audience**
Knowing the specific demographic you're targeting enables you to tailor content, language, and tone to match viewer preferences. Defining your audience also helps inform other aspects of content creation, such as video length and style.

o **Analysing Demographic Data**: Demographic tools on YouTube and platforms like Pew Research Center provide insights into viewer ages, interests, and regional trends, allowing for better audience targeting.

o **Tailoring Content for Specific Age Groups**: Content style varies by age group. For instance, younger audiences on TikTok prefer fast-paced, humorous videos, while older viewers on YouTube might appreciate in-depth tutorials or thought-provoking content.

o **Creating a Viewer Persona**: Building a "persona" for your average viewer can guide content decisions. A persona includes demographic details (age, location, interests) and viewing habits, helping to create videos that meet viewers' expectations.

3. **Developing a Unique Content Angle**
Standing out on YouTube requires a unique approach. This might mean combining topics (e.g., "sustainable fashion for tech enthusiasts") or delivering content in a distinctive format, such as animated explainer videos.

o **Combining Multiple Interests**: Combining interests can carve out a unique niche. For example, a channel that merges personal finance with travel tips appeals to budget-conscious travellers, a popular audience in the USA and Europe.

- o **Exploring Different Formats**: Formats such as live streams, tutorials, or vlogs each have unique engagement potential. Testing formats early on helps identify what resonates best with your audience.

- o **Using Branding Elements**: Consistent branding, including logos, intros, and colour schemes, creates a memorable channel identity. A strong brand identity helps build recognition and loyalty among viewers.

2.4.2 Monetisation Methods: Ads, Sponsorships, and Memberships

Once your channel begins to grow, implementing multiple revenue streams allows you to maximise income. YouTube offers various monetisation options, each with specific eligibility requirements and earning potential.

1. **Earning Through YouTube Ads**
   Ads are the primary income source for many YouTubers. The YouTube Partner Programme (YPP) enables creators to earn from ads, but eligibility requires meeting specific milestones, such as 1,000 subscribers and 4,000 watch hours.

   - o **Types of YouTube Ads**: YouTube provides several ad formats, including skippable, non-skippable, and overlay ads. Each format offers different earning potential, depending on the viewer's engagement and geography.

   - o **Maximising Ad Revenue**: Channels with high watch times and viewer retention tend to generate higher ad revenue. For example, longer videos can include multiple ads, increasing revenue per video.

- ○ **Ad Revenue Across Regions**: Ad revenue varies by region, with creators in the USA often earning higher CPM (cost per thousand views) rates compared to those in other regions. Understanding these variations can help set realistic income expectations.

2. **Attracting Sponsorships and Brand Deals**
Sponsorships are a lucrative income source, especially for creators in niches with high commercial appeal. Brands pay creators to feature products in videos, providing income beyond ad revenue.

- ○ **Reaching Out to Brands**: Networking platforms like Grapevine, AspireIQ, and Influencity connect creators with potential sponsors. Pitching brands that align with your audience increases the likelihood of securing sponsorships.

- ○ **Creating Authentic Sponsored Content**: Successful sponsored content feels genuine and aligns with a channel's usual style. For example, a travel vlogger might showcase travel-related products, ensuring the promotion resonates with viewers.

- ○ **Setting Sponsorship Rates**: Sponsorship rates vary by audience size, niche, and engagement rate. Researching market rates and negotiating terms allows creators to maximise earnings and build sustainable brand relationships.

3. **Engaging Viewers Through Memberships and Exclusive Content**
Membership programmes allow creators to offer exclusive content to subscribers in exchange for a monthly fee. YouTube's Memberships feature, along

with third-party platforms like Patreon, provides a recurring income stream.

- **Creating Tiered Membership Benefits**: Tiered memberships offer exclusive perks, such as behind-the-scenes content, live Q&A sessions, or early access to videos. These benefits create value and encourage viewers to support the channel.

- **Promoting Memberships Strategically**: Mentioning memberships in videos, descriptions, and social media posts can encourage sign-ups without overwhelming non-members.

- **Building a Loyal Community**: Memberships foster a sense of exclusivity and community. Engaging with members through comments, special streams, or Discord servers strengthens relationships and loyalty.

2.4.3 Growing Subscribers and Viewer Engagement

Subscriber growth and viewer engagement are crucial for YouTube success. More subscribers mean a larger potential audience for each video, while engagement metrics like likes, comments, and shares increase visibility in YouTube's algorithm.

1. **Optimising Content for YouTube's Algorithm**
   YouTube's algorithm prioritises videos that attract high watch times and engagement. Optimising content for these metrics boosts the likelihood of appearing in search results and suggested videos.

   - **Creating Engaging Thumbnails and Titles**: Eye-catching thumbnails and clickable titles are essential for attracting viewers. A/B testing thumbnails and using keywords in titles can increase click-through rates.

- o **Improving Viewer Retention**: YouTube rewards high viewer retention, so keeping viewers engaged from start to finish is essential. Starting videos with a hook and minimising filler content helps maintain interest.

- o **Understanding YouTube Analytics**: YouTube Analytics provides insights into viewer demographics, engagement rates, and watch times. Analysing this data helps identify trends and optimise content accordingly.

2. **Encouraging Interaction and Community Building**
   Building an active community encourages viewer loyalty and increases the likelihood of repeat views. Engaged subscribers are also more likely to support monetisation efforts, such as memberships or merchandise.

   - o **Replying to Comments and Questions**: Replying to viewer comments creates a personal connection and shows appreciation. Acknowledging viewer input fosters loyalty and encourages further interaction.

   - o **Using Calls to Action (CTAs)**: CTAs like "Subscribe for more" or "Let me know your thoughts in the comments" encourage interaction. These small prompts remind viewers to engage, boosting visibility and subscriber growth.

   - o **Hosting Live Streams and Q&As**: Live streams provide an opportunity for real-time engagement, strengthening the bond between creator and audience. Many creators use live sessions to answer questions, discuss upcoming projects, or chat with fans.

3. **Collaborating with Other Creators**
   Collaboration with other YouTubers exposes a channel to new audiences, driving subscriber growth. Partnerships with creators in complementary niches

allow both channels to benefit from each other's viewership.

- o **Cross-Promotional Content**: Collaborative videos, where creators co-host or appear on each other's channels, introduce both audiences to new content. This method often leads to a surge in subscribers.

- o **Guest Appearances and Feature Videos**: Many creators invite guests for interviews or feature videos, adding variety to their content and attracting the guest's audience.

- o **Networking and Building Connections**: Engaging with other YouTubers in comments, forums, and industry events fosters relationships that lead to potential collaborations. Networking strengthens a channel's presence within the community.

Conclusion

Building a profitable YouTube channel involves strategic planning, creative content, and consistent audience engagement. By choosing a unique focus, utilising multiple monetisation methods, and actively growing subscriber engagement, creators can transform their channels into sustainable sources of income. Success on YouTube is driven by both the quality of content and the strength of viewer relationships, making authenticity and audience connection essential components.

In the next section, we'll explore additional digital platforms and strategies for online income generation, specifically focusing on **social media** as a profitable avenue for building a personal brand, engaging with audiences, and diversifying revenue streams. From mastering platform-specific content to maximising income through sponsorships, affiliate marketing, and product sales, this guide will provide readers with the actionable steps needed to make social media a viable source of income.

2.5 Social Media for Profit

Social media is a powerful tool for creating income online, offering a range of monetisation options from sponsored posts and affiliate marketing to selling digital products. With its fast-paced, interactive nature, social media is ideal for creators who thrive on direct engagement with their audience. This section will explore strategies for building a profitable social media presence by choosing the right platforms, growing an engaged following, and utilising monetisation techniques effectively.

2.5.1 Choosing the Right Social Media Platform

Selecting the appropriate social media platform is key to reaching your target audience and establishing a profitable brand. Each platform has its strengths, user demographics, and unique features, making it important to align your content style with the platform best suited to your niche.

1. **Platform-Specific Demographics and Strengths**
   Different platforms attract varied demographics, and understanding these preferences helps tailor content and monetisation strategies to meet audience expectations.

   o **Instagram's Visual Appeal**: Instagram is popular for visually engaging content, ideal for niches like fashion, food, travel, and lifestyle. Its core audience includes young adults across the USA, UK, and Europe, making it suitable for brands targeting a wide age range.

   o **TikTok's Viral Potential**: Known for its short-form videos and viral trends, TikTok is highly popular among Gen Z users globally. Content that's fast-paced, humorous, or trend-driven tends to perform well on this platform, especially for creators in entertainment, fashion, or fitness niches.

- o **Twitter's Conversational Focus**: Twitter is effective for news, discussion, and thought leadership, often used by brands and professionals in tech, finance, and politics. It's ideal for those who enjoy engaging in real-time conversations and sharing insights.

2. **Assessing Content Fit for Each Platform**
The content format and tone vary significantly by platform, so choosing one that aligns with your style and goals is essential for attracting and retaining followers.

   - o **Instagram's Visual-Driven Content**: High-quality photos, Stories, and Reels work well on Instagram, allowing creators to showcase aesthetics and creativity. This platform is particularly effective for showcasing products and curated lifestyles.

   - o **Educational and Short-Form Content on TikTok**: TikTok's algorithm rewards short, engaging videos, making it suitable for tutorials, tips, and challenges. It's an excellent platform for educational niches, such as cooking tips, financial advice, or workout routines.

   - o **Twitter's Engagement Through Threads and Polls**: Twitter is ideal for engaging followers through threaded discussions, polls, and live tweeting. It's effective for brands that want to build a following around industry insights, opinions, and breaking news.

3. **Evaluating Monetisation Potential by Platform**
Each social media platform offers unique monetisation options. Understanding these options helps creators maximise revenue based on the platform they choose.

   - o **Instagram's Sponsored Content and Affiliate Marketing**: Instagram is one of the most profitable platforms for sponsored posts and affiliate marketing, especially for creators with an engaged audience in consumer-oriented niches.

- o **TikTok's Creator Fund and Sponsorships**: TikTok's Creator Fund pays eligible creators based on views, while brand sponsorships offer significant earning potential, particularly for content that goes viral.

- o **Twitter's Affiliate Links and Promotion Opportunities**: Although Twitter lacks direct monetisation features, it's effective for affiliate marketing and driving traffic to other sites, such as blogs or e-commerce pages.

2.5.2 Growing an Engaged Audience

Building a loyal, engaged following is essential for profitable social media. Followers who feel connected to your brand are more likely to engage with content, support monetisation efforts, and promote your page to new audiences.

1. **Creating Authentic and Valuable Content**
   Authenticity is key on social media, as followers are more likely to engage with creators who share genuine insights and value-driven content. Each post should aim to entertain, educate, or inspire.

   - o **Storytelling for Connection**: Storytelling builds a personal connection, whether through personal anecdotes or behind-the-scenes insights. This approach resonates well across platforms, particularly for Instagram and Twitter.

   - o **Consistency and Value in Content**: Posting regularly and focusing on valuable content, such as tutorials, tips, or inspirational posts, helps attract a loyal audience. For example, a fitness influencer might share weekly workout routines or healthy recipes to keep followers engaged.

- **Balancing Promotional and Personal Content**: While monetisation is essential, over-promotion can alienate followers. A balanced approach, mixing promotional posts with personal or value-based content, fosters trust and engagement.

2. **Utilising Platform-Specific Features**
Each platform offers unique features designed to enhance engagement. Using these tools strategically can boost visibility and encourage interaction.

- **Instagram's Stories, Reels, and IGTV**: Instagram Stories offer an informal way to connect with followers, while Reels and IGTV provide additional content formats for engaging audiences with short videos and live interactions.

- **TikTok's Trends and Hashtags**: Leveraging TikTok's hashtag challenges and trending sounds can increase visibility. Participating in trending challenges or creating branded hashtags encourages followers to engage and share.

- **Twitter's Polls and Q&A Threads**: Twitter's poll feature and Q&A threads allow creators to interact with followers in real-time. Polls are ideal for gauging interests, while Q&A threads create an interactive experience that strengthens community.

3. **Interacting Directly with Followers**
Engaging directly with followers helps create a loyal community. Personal responses, shout-outs, and acknowledging feedback foster a sense of belonging and encourage ongoing interaction.

- **Replying to Comments and Messages**: Acknowledging comments and direct messages demonstrates appreciation for follower support.

Engaging in conversations creates stronger connections and builds trust.

- o **Hosting Q&A Sessions and Live Streams**: Q&A sessions and live streams on Instagram or TikTok allow followers to interact in real-time. Answering questions and addressing comments directly makes followers feel valued.

- o **Community-Centric Content**: Sharing user-generated content or featuring followers in posts reinforces a sense of community. For example, a fashion influencer might showcase followers wearing their recommended outfits.

2.5.3 Monetising Social Media Content

Once a following is established, social media can be monetised through various methods, including sponsorships, affiliate marketing, and selling digital products. Each monetisation option suits different types of content and audience preferences.

1. **Sponsored Content and Brand Collaborations**
   Sponsored posts and brand collaborations are profitable options, allowing creators to partner with companies that align with their niche and audience.

   - o **Finding Suitable Brand Partnerships**: Partnering with brands that match your content and audience demographics is crucial. Platforms like AspireIQ, Influencity, and BrandSnob connect creators with brands seeking sponsorships.

   - o **Creating Authentic Sponsored Posts**: Successful sponsored content feels authentic. Integrating products naturally into posts and sharing genuine feedback ensures promotions resonate with followers.

- o **Negotiating Fair Sponsorship Rates**: Sponsorship rates vary by audience size, engagement, and niche. Researching market rates and setting clear terms ensures sustainable, fair partnerships.

2. **Affiliate Marketing for Passive Income**
Affiliate marketing allows creators to earn commissions by promoting products through unique links. This method is effective for creators with audiences interested in product recommendations.

   - o **Selecting Affiliate Programmes and Products**: Platforms like Amazon Associates, ShareASale, and Rakuten offer affiliate programmes across various niches. Selecting products relevant to your content ensures recommendations are credible.

   - o **Embedding Affiliate Links**: Links can be strategically placed in Instagram Stories (with swipe-up links for verified accounts), video descriptions on TikTok, or as pinned tweets on Twitter.

   - o **Disclosure for Transparency**: Disclosing affiliate links fosters trust and complies with legal guidelines in the USA, UK, and EU. Transparent disclosure encourages followers to support recommendations.

3. **Selling Digital Products and Personalised Services**
Many creators diversify income by selling digital products, such as e-books, online courses, or consulting services. This approach leverages expertise and creates additional revenue streams.

   - o **Creating E-Books or Guides**: E-books or downloadable guides are popular digital products in niches like health, finance, and lifestyle. They allow followers to gain in-depth knowledge and support the creator's work.

- o **Offering Online Courses and Workshops**: For creators with specialised skills, online courses or workshops provide valuable educational content. Platforms like Teachable and Thinkific make it easy to host and sell courses.

- o **Consulting and Personalised Services**: One-on-one consulting or personalised services, such as social media audits or wellness coaching, enable creators to offer tailored advice. This method works well for creators with high expertise in specific areas.

Conclusion

Social media offers numerous monetisation pathways, from brand partnerships and affiliate marketing to selling digital products. By choosing the right platform, engaging with followers, and using multiple revenue streams, creators can turn their social media presence into a sustainable source of income. Success in social media monetisation requires a blend of consistency, creativity, and audience-focused strategies, ensuring long-term engagement and profitability.

3. Social Media Influencing and Marketing

Social media influencing has become one of the most effective ways to reach audiences and generate income through brand collaborations, paid posts, and digital content creation. This section provides a guide for establishing an influencing career, from choosing the right platforms to crafting engaging content and maximising monetisation opportunities. We'll look at platform-specific strategies and insights into best practices for creating and sustaining a profitable influence.

3.1 Platforms: Instagram, TikTok, Twitter, and More

Choosing the right platform is crucial for influencers, as each platform has its audience, strengths, and monetisation potential. By selecting platforms that best align with your content style and audience preferences, you can optimise your reach and engagement.

1. **Instagram: The Visual Marketing Hub**
   Instagram remains a leading platform for influencers due to its strong visual emphasis and high engagement. Known for its aesthetic appeal, it is well-suited to niches such as fashion, food, fitness, and lifestyle.

   o **Leveraging Instagram Stories and Reels**: Instagram Stories offer a behind-the-scenes look, allowing influencers to connect informally with followers. Reels provide opportunities for short, engaging videos that can reach a broader audience through the Explore page.

   o **Target Audience and Demographics**: Instagram's core demographic is young adults, particularly those aged 18–34. In the UK and Europe, this platform is popular among urban millennials, making it ideal for products or services targeting this age group.

- o **Instagram Shopping and Shoppable Posts**: Instagram's shopping features allow influencers to tag products directly in their posts, enabling seamless purchasing experiences. This feature is especially useful for influencers in e-commerce and retail.

2. **TikTok: Viral Potential and Short-Form Content**
TikTok's rapid growth has made it a powerhouse for influencers, particularly those targeting Gen Z. Its short-form video format encourages creativity, humour, and virality, making it ideal for dynamic, fast-paced content.

- o **Trends, Hashtags, and Challenges**: TikTok's algorithm rewards content that participates in trending challenges and hashtags. By leveraging these trends, influencers can expand their reach and potentially go viral.

- o **Influencing Younger Audiences**: TikTok has a predominantly young audience, with a strong presence among users aged 16–24. In the USA, UK, and Europe, brands targeting younger consumers often prioritise TikTok collaborations.

- o **TikTok Creator Fund and Brand Partnerships**: TikTok's Creator Fund offers eligible influencers income based on video views, while brand partnerships allow for sponsored posts. These monetisation options enable creators to generate income through both organic and sponsored content.

3. **Twitter: Real-Time Engagement and Thought Leadership**
While not as visually oriented as Instagram or TikTok, Twitter is ideal for influencers focused on news, insights, and real-time interaction. Twitter's format supports text-heavy content, ideal for thought leadership and commentary.

- ○ **Engaging Through Threads and Discussions**: Twitter threads allow influencers to share insights, tell stories, or provide commentary on current events. This feature is particularly valuable for influencers in industries like tech, finance, and politics.

- ○ **Using Polls and Q&A Sessions**: Polls and Q&A sessions increase interaction with followers, allowing influencers to gain insights into their audience's preferences or involve them in discussions.

- ○ **Driving Traffic to Other Platforms**: Twitter is effective for directing followers to other platforms, such as blogs, YouTube channels, or Instagram profiles. Influencers often use Twitter as a central hub for updates and cross-promotion.

3.2 Creating Engaging Content

High-quality, engaging content is essential for maintaining audience interest and building a loyal following. Successful influencers are consistent, authentic, and skilled at creating content that resonates with their target audience.

1. **Defining Your Content Strategy**
   A clear content strategy allows influencers to create posts that align with their brand and audience preferences. The strategy should outline content types, posting frequency, and engagement goals.

   - ○ **Identifying Core Content Pillars**: Content pillars are topics or themes that represent an influencer's brand. For instance, a fitness influencer might focus on workout routines, nutrition, and mental wellness.

   - ○ **Balancing Content Types**: Mixing content types—such as informative, entertaining, and promotional posts—keeps followers engaged. Educational "how-to" posts, personal stories, and product reviews provide variety.

- o **Setting a Consistent Posting Schedule**: Consistency is key to maintaining follower engagement. Most platforms reward regular posting, and having a content calendar helps streamline the process.

2. **Storytelling for Authenticity**
Authentic storytelling helps influencers build a personal connection with their followers. This connection fosters trust, making audiences more receptive to both organic and sponsored content.

- o **Sharing Personal Stories**: Followers appreciate influencers who share relatable or inspiring stories. Personal anecdotes, challenges, and milestones give followers a sense of connection.

- o **Incorporating Behind-the-Scenes Content**: Behind-the-scenes posts, such as daily routines or behind-the-scenes looks at projects, make influencers appear more relatable and genuine.

- o **Showcasing Brand Partnerships Authentically**: Authenticity is crucial when promoting sponsored content. Influencers should choose partnerships that align with their values and style, integrating promotions naturally into their content.

3. **Engaging Through Interactive Content**
Interactive content encourages audience participation, increasing engagement and fostering a sense of community. Platforms like Instagram and TikTok offer tools specifically designed for interaction.

- o **Using Polls, Quizzes, and Q&A Features**: Instagram Stories and Twitter offer interactive tools like polls and quizzes that invite follower

115

input, providing insights into their preferences and interests.

- o **Hosting Live Streams**: Live streaming on Instagram or TikTok allows for real-time interaction, whether through Q&A sessions, tutorials, or special events. Live sessions create an authentic and immediate connection.

- o **Creating Challenges and Hashtags**: Influencers can create their own challenges or branded hashtags to encourage user-generated content. This approach expands reach, as followers engage with and share the content with their networks.

3.3 Monetisation through Brand Collaborations and Paid Posts

Monetisation on social media can be achieved through collaborations with brands, paid posts, affiliate marketing, and more. A diverse monetisation strategy maximises earning potential and creates sustainable income streams.

1. **Brand Collaborations and Sponsored Posts**
   Brand collaborations are a primary income source for influencers. Brands pay influencers to feature products or services in posts, often in the form of sponsored content, reviews, or product placements.

   - o **Identifying Relevant Brand Partnerships**: Partnering with brands that align with an influencer's niche and values ensures that collaborations feel authentic. For example, a beauty influencer might partner with skincare or makeup brands.

   - o **Negotiating Sponsorship Terms**: Influencers should establish terms that outline post requirements, timelines, and payment. Platforms like AspireIQ and BrandSnob help connect

influencers with brands, simplifying the
negotiation process.

- o **Maintaining Authenticity in Sponsored Content**: Authenticity is crucial for maintaining trust. Integrating products naturally into content and providing genuine feedback ensures followers remain engaged with sponsored posts.

2. **Affiliate Marketing for Passive Income**
   Affiliate marketing allows influencers to earn commissions by promoting products through unique links. This method is especially effective for influencers in niches with high product demand, such as fashion, tech, and beauty.

   - o **Choosing Affiliate Programmes and Products**: Selecting programmes that offer products relevant to an influencer's niche is essential. Amazon Associates, RewardStyle, and ShareASale are popular options for various niches.

   - o **Embedding Affiliate Links in Posts and Stories**: Platforms like Instagram allow influencers to include affiliate links in Stories (for verified accounts), captions, or profiles. Consistent promotion across multiple platforms increases clicks.

   - o **Transparency and Legal Compliance**: Disclosure is essential for trust and legal compliance in the USA, UK, and Europe. Clearly labelling affiliate links ensures followers know when a post contains promotional content.

3. **Creating and Selling Digital Products or Services**
   Many influencers diversify income by creating and selling digital products or services, such as e-books, online courses, or consulting. This approach leverages expertise and provides value to followers while generating income.

- o **E-Books, Guides, and Courses**: E-books or online courses allow influencers to share in-depth knowledge. For example, a wellness influencer might sell a meal-planning guide, while a finance influencer offers a budgeting course.

- o **Personalised Services**: Influencers with specific expertise, such as fitness coaching or business consulting, can offer one-on-one services. These services add value for followers seeking tailored advice.

- o **Utilising Platforms for Sales**: Digital product platforms like Etsy, Gumroad, and Teachable make it easy for influencers to host and sell products, providing a straightforward setup for monetisation.

Conclusion

Social media influencing and marketing provide numerous income opportunities, from brand collaborations to creating and selling digital products. By choosing the right platforms, creating engaging content, and leveraging multiple monetisation strategies, influencers can turn their social media presence into a sustainable business. Success requires a commitment to authenticity, consistency, and audience engagement, building a loyal following that supports long-term growth and profitability.

4. Leveraging Online Courses and Webinars

Online courses and webinars are powerful tools for income generation, knowledge sharing, and establishing authority. This section delves into creating and selling digital courses, building authority in a niche, and using webinars to boost engagement and drive sales. By incorporating real-world examples, regional insights, and practical strategies, we'll provide readers with an in-depth, actionable guide.

4.1 Creating and Selling Digital Courses

Creating a successful digital course requires careful planning, from designing content that meets audience needs to selecting a suitable platform and implementing effective pricing strategies. This subsection will break down each essential element to guide readers in launching profitable courses.

1. **Planning Your Course Content and Structure**

A structured approach to course content ensures value and clarity for students. This subsection will offer a step-by-step guide to planning topics, structuring modules, and selecting multimedia formats to enhance learning experiences.

- o **Identifying Audience Needs and Demand Analysis**
  Researching audience interests, needs, and gaps in the market is essential to choosing profitable course topics. Tools like Google Trends and Udemy's Marketplace Insights can help pinpoint high-demand topics across the USA, UK, and European markets.

  - **Market-Specific Demand**: Consider trends in digital marketing for the USA, language learning for Europe, or wellness niches in the UK.

- **Surveying Your Audience**: Polling potential students or engaging them in social media Q&A can reveal valuable insights.

- **Competitive Analysis**: Studying competitors' courses helps identify unique angles or content gaps, ensuring your course stands out.

o **Designing Course Modules and Lessons**
Structuring the course into logical modules provides clarity and progress tracking for students. Each module should build on the previous one, gradually advancing students through the material.

- **Creating Learning Objectives**: Define clear goals for each module, ensuring content aligns with overall objectives.

- **Mixing Content Types for Engagement**: Video lectures, downloadable worksheets, quizzes, and case studies enhance engagement and comprehension.

- **Testing Content with Beta Groups**: Engaging a small audience to test content provides feedback, helping refine modules for clarity and value.

o **Choosing a Format (Video, Text, or Multimedia)**
Selecting the right format based on audience preference and course goals is crucial. Video-based courses are popular for hands-on topics, while text-based content may suit theory-heavy subjects.

- **Live vs. Pre-Recorded Video**: Live video fosters interaction, while pre-recorded material offers flexibility.

- **Interactive Content for Enhanced Learning**: Adding quizzes, assignments, and group discussions boosts engagement and retention.

- **Adapting for Accessibility**: Including captions for videos and providing transcripts ensures accessibility for diverse learners.

2. Choosing the Right Platform for Hosting

Selecting a platform impacts visibility, accessibility, and functionality. Here, we'll discuss options from dedicated platforms to self-hosting and social media integration, along with the pros and cons of each.

- **Dedicated Course Platforms: Teachable, Thinkific, Udemy**
  Dedicated platforms provide easy setup, integrated marketing tools, and a built-in audience.

  o **Comparing Pricing and Features**: Each platform offers different commission structures and pricing tiers.

  o **Utilising Built-In Marketing Tools**: Teachable and Thinkific offer email marketing and sales tracking, simplifying promotions.

  o **Advantages of Platform-Based Audiences**: Udemy's marketplace can increase visibility, especially in the USA and Europe.

- **Self-Hosting with WordPress or LMS Plugins**
  Self-hosting provides control over content, branding, and pricing, ideal for creators who want independence.

- Using WordPress Plugins (e.g., LearnDash):
  LMS plugins enable course creation on personal
  websites, providing customisation.

- Protecting Content with Membership
  Plugins: Plugins like MemberPress restrict
  access to enrolled students, ensuring exclusivity.

- Integrating Payment Gateways: Options like
  Stripe and PayPal offer secure payment
  processing, essential for reaching global
  audiences.

- **Social Media Platforms as Course Launch Pads**
  Social media channels such as Instagram, LinkedIn, and
  Facebook can serve as promotional platforms, driving
  traffic to hosted courses.

  - Instagram Stories and LinkedIn for Teasers:
    Short, engaging previews attract interest.

  - Facebook Groups for Community-Building:
    Private groups foster engagement and build
    anticipation for new courses.

  - Cross-Promotional Content: Using multiple
    channels to reach diverse audiences increases
    enrolment rates.

3. Pricing and Marketing Your Course

Choosing the right pricing model and marketing strategy can
significantly impact course enrolment and revenue. This
subsection will detail approaches to setting prices, creating a
marketing funnel, and utilising special offers to boost sales.

- **Determining Pricing Models**
  Pricing can be structured as a one-time purchase,
  subscription, or pay-per-module.

- o **Competitive Pricing Analysis**: Reviewing similar courses in each market ensures pricing is attractive.

- o **Offering Tiered Access**: Premium, standard, and basic options cater to different budgets.

- o **Testing Introductory Pricing**: Launching with an introductory price encourages initial enrolments.

- **Developing a Marketing Funnel**
A marketing funnel nurtures potential students from awareness to purchase, often through free content, nurturing emails, and social proof.

  - o **Lead Generation through Free Resources**: Offering a free lesson or e-book draws in leads.

  - o **Email Marketing for Conversion**: A series of emails reinforces course value and addresses objections.

  - o **Leveraging Testimonials and Social Proof**: Displaying success stories builds credibility.

- **Offering Discounts and Early Bird Deals**
Promotions, such as limited-time discounts or bonus content, create urgency and encourage enrolments.

  - o **Seasonal Discounts**: Offering discounts around holidays or back-to-school seasons drives enrolment.

  - o **Group Enrolment Discounts**: Offering reduced rates for multiple sign-ups can increase sales volume.

  - o **Bundling Courses with Added Value**: Bundling courses or including bonus material provides additional incentives.

4.2 Building Authority in Your Niche

Establishing authority is essential for attracting students and differentiating your course. This section provides strategies for building credibility through quality content, engagement, and social proof.

---

1. Creating High-Quality, Valuable Content

Quality content is fundamental to establishing authority. This involves offering actionable insights, case studies, and regularly updating content to reflect industry developments.

- **Providing Actionable Insights and Skills**
  Courses should deliver tangible takeaways that students can apply immediately.

  - **Step-by-Step Guides and Examples**: Clear guides simplify complex topics, enhancing comprehension.

  - **Including Practical Exercises**: Activities that reinforce learning outcomes improve student success.

  - **Customising Content for Different Markets**: Localised examples or case studies increase relevance.

- **Incorporating Case Studies and Real-World Examples**
  Relevant examples enhance credibility, particularly in fields like business or technology.

  - **Case Studies of Successful Businesses or Projects**: Showcasing real-world applications builds authority.

  - **Inviting Guest Experts for Interviews**: Featuring industry experts broadens perspective and adds credibility.

- **Illustrating Concepts through Success Stories**: Personal success stories resonate well with students.

  o **Staying Updated on Industry Trends**
  Keeping courses current with trends is crucial for ongoing relevance and credibility.

  - **Regular Content Updates**: Updating material annually keeps courses relevant.

  - **Adding Emerging Topics**: Covering new trends, like AI in tech courses, adds value.

  - **Offering Continuing Education Units (CEUs)**: Accrediting courses provides additional credibility, appealing to professionals.

2. Engaging with Your Audience Across Platforms

Expanding your presence across platforms builds recognition and helps connect with prospective students, enhancing reputation in the field.

  o **Providing Free Content on Social Media**
  Sharing valuable insights on platforms like LinkedIn or Instagram previews your expertise.

  - **Weekly Tips or Tutorials**: Posting regular insights attracts and nurtures followers.

  - **Creating Interactive Content**: Polls and Q&A sessions encourage audience interaction.

  - **Showcasing Success Stories and Testimonials**: Sharing testimonials builds trust.

- o **Hosting Q&A Sessions, Webinars, or Live Streams**
  Live interactions allow real-time engagement, enhancing trust and demonstrating expertise.

  - **Scheduling Monthly Q&A Sessions**: Regular sessions keep your audience engaged.

  - **Webinars on Trending Topics**: Presenting current topics attracts industry interest.

  - **Offering Free Webinars as Previews**: Previews build excitement for full courses.

- o **Networking with Industry Peers and Influencers**
  Collaborating with other experts widens reach and boosts authority.

  - **Guest Blog Posts and Cross-Promotion**: Sharing platforms introduces you to new audiences.

  - **Panel Discussions or Roundtable Webinars**: Joint sessions expand exposure.

  - **Engagement with Industry Forums**: Active participation in discussions showcases knowledge.

---

3. **Gathering Testimonials and Social Proof**

Social proof, such as testimonials and case studies, builds credibility, encouraging new students to enrol.

- o **Requesting Testimonials from Students and Clients**

Positive feedback enhances credibility and reassures potential students.

- **Providing Incentives for Reviews**: Discounted rates or bonuses encourage testimonials.

- **Highlighting Detailed Reviews**: Featuring in-depth feedback builds trust.

- **Using Video Testimonials for Authenticity**: Video testimonials increase relatability.

- **Leveraging Case Studies and Success Stories** Demonstrating real-world success shows the practical impact of your courses.

  - **Following Up with Successful Students**: Keeping in touch with students highlights long-term impact.

  - **Publishing Success Metrics**: Sharing quantifiable achievements validates your course's efficacy.

  - **Documenting Career Progression Stories**: Highlighting students' professional growth strengthens credibility.

- **Utilising Platform Reviews and Ratings** Reviews on course platforms increase visibility and credibility.

  - **Encouraging Reviews on Platforms like Udemy or Teachable**: Higher ratings improve platform positioning.

  - **Responding to Feedback**: Acknowledging feedback, even critical, shows commitment to improvement.

- **Featuring Ratings on Social Media**: Sharing positive ratings extends reach to a broader audience.

4.3 Using Webinars for Engagement and Sales

Webinars are a powerful tool for showcasing expertise, connecting with audiences in real time, and converting interested attendees into paying students. By planning relevant topics, promoting effectively, and implementing a structured follow-up strategy, webinars can be a highly effective sales channel.

1. **Planning Webinar Topics and Format**

Thoughtful planning is essential to delivering a webinar that captivates and engages attendees. Choosing relevant topics, creating a structured presentation, and determining the format all contribute to the overall success of the session.

- o **Selecting Topics Aligned with Audience Needs**
  To attract a targeted audience, choose webinar topics that align closely with their interests and needs. Understanding common questions, pain points, and trending subjects within your niche can guide topic selection.

  - **Identifying High-Interest Topics**: Use surveys, social media polls, or feedback from past course participants to determine what your audience wants to learn.

  - **Market-Specific Topics**: Consider regional preferences; for example, personal finance for US audiences, language learning for Europe, or tech skills for the UK.

- **Aligning with Course Content**: Choose topics that provide a preview of your course, making it easy for attendees to see how the webinar content relates to your full offering.

o **Deciding Between Live vs. Pre-Recorded Webinars**
Each format offers distinct advantages. Live webinars allow for real-time interaction and a sense of immediacy, while pre-recorded webinars can be made available on-demand, allowing attendees to join at their convenience.

- **Live Webinars for Real-Time Q&A**: Engaging with attendees during live sessions builds trust and allows for immediate feedback.

- **On-Demand Webinars for Flexibility**: Recorded webinars that can be accessed anytime increase reach, especially for global audiences.

- **Hybrid Options**: Some creators use pre-recorded presentations with a live Q&A at the end, combining the advantages of both formats.

o **Creating a Structured, Professional Presentation**
A well-organised presentation keeps attendees engaged and conveys professionalism. Each segment of the webinar should be clear, purposeful, and flow smoothly.

- **Dividing the Webinar into Sections**: Structure your content with an introduction, main points, and a conclusion to keep it focused.

- **Using Visuals for Clarity**: Slides, graphics, and infographics enhance comprehension, especially for complex topics.

- **Interactive Features**: Include polls, quizzes, or prompts to comment, making the webinar more interactive and engaging.

2. Promoting Your Webinar Effectively

To maximise attendance, webinar promotion should be strategic and targeted. Leveraging multiple channels, crafting engaging promotional materials, and creating incentives for early registration are all effective techniques for attracting attendees.

- **Utilising Email Marketing to Drive Registrations**
  Email marketing is a reliable tool for reaching a targeted audience and encouraging registrations. With personalised messaging, emails can build excitement and provide essential information leading up to the event.

  - **Segmenting Your Email List**: Segmenting lists by interest or location helps tailor messages, increasing the relevance of the invitation.

  - **Automated Reminders for Registered Attendees**: Scheduling reminder emails 24 hours and 1 hour before the event can boost attendance.

  - **Offering a Teaser**: Share a sneak peek of the webinar content in your email invites to spark interest.

- **Leveraging Social Media Platforms for Wider Reach**

Promoting webinars on social media can expand reach, especially when targeting specific demographics on platforms like Instagram, LinkedIn, and Twitter.

- **Creating Engaging Graphics and Captions**: Design visually appealing posts with clear webinar details and a compelling call to action.

- **Using Paid Ads for Targeted Promotion**: Running ads on Facebook or Instagram allows you to target specific demographics and increase sign-ups.

- **Encouraging Shares**: Add a call-to-action encouraging followers to share the post, increasing reach and visibility.

o **Incentivising Early Registrations**
  Offering exclusive content, discounts, or access to a bonus guide for early registrants can create urgency and boost initial sign-ups.

  - **Discount Codes for Related Products**: Offer a discount on related courses or e-books as a perk for registering early.

  - **Exclusive Content Access**: Providing downloadable guides or checklists for registrants adds immediate value.

  - **VIP Access to a Post-Webinar Q&A**: Letting early registrants participate in a more personal, post-webinar Q&A creates a feeling of exclusivity.

---

3. **Converting Webinar Attendees into Students**

Converting attendees into paying students requires a well-planned approach, from highlighting course benefits during the webinar to following up with personalised messages. This subsection details the steps to maximise conversions and turn interest into enrolment.

- o **Highlighting Course Benefits Throughout the Webinar**
  Subtly introduce the value of your course during the presentation, allowing attendees to see how the course builds on the webinar content. A structured approach to mentioning benefits keeps the pitch low-key yet effective.

  - **Showcasing Relevant Course Modules**: Highlight specific modules in the course that expand on webinar topics.

  - **Sharing Success Stories**: Mention past student successes to illustrate the course's value.

  - **Answering Common Course Questions**: Address FAQs about the course directly in the webinar, alleviating concerns and making enrolment easier.

- o **Offering a Time-Limited Discount or Bonus for Attendees**
  Providing a time-sensitive discount or adding value through bonus content encourages quick action from attendees.

  - **Limited-Time Discount Code**: Offering a discount valid for 48 hours after the webinar creates a sense of urgency.

  - **Bonus Module or One-on-One Session**: Including an exclusive bonus module or a free consultation incentivises sign-ups.

- **Referral Discounts for Bringing Friends**: Allowing attendees to refer friends at a discounted rate can multiply conversions.

o **Sending Follow-Up Emails to Attendees**
Follow-up emails reinforce the benefits of the course, provide additional information, and gently nudge attendees toward enrolment.

- **Thank-You Email with a Recap**: A thank-you email with a summary of key points reminds attendees of the webinar's value.

- **Reminder of the Limited-Time Offer**: A follow-up email reminding them of the discount or bonus maintains urgency.

- **Personalised Outreach for High-Engagement Attendees**: Identify attendees who asked questions or participated actively, and reach out with a personalised message.

Conclusion

Online courses and webinars are highly effective tools for generating income, establishing authority, and engaging with a global audience. By focusing on quality content, authenticity, and consistent engagement, course creators and educators can develop sustainable revenue streams while providing valuable learning experiences. Success in leveraging online courses and webinars requires a deep understanding of audience needs, thoughtful planning, and a commitment to delivering genuine value.

In the next chapter, we will explore the world of **E-commerce and Dropshipping**, providing readers with a comprehensive guide to setting up online stores, managing logistics, and building a scalable retail business. This chapter will offer actionable strategies for achieving profitability and navigating the unique challenges of e-commerce.

Chapter 3: E-Commerce and Dropshipping

E-commerce has transformed the way businesses operate, allowing individuals and companies to sell products globally without the limitations of a physical storefront. Among the various e-commerce approaches, dropshipping has gained popularity for its low barrier to entry and scalability. This chapter explores the fundamental e-commerce business models, guides readers in selecting the most suitable approach, and provides insights into managing logistics and fulfilment effectively. By understanding these principles, aspiring entrepreneurs can build sustainable, profitable e-commerce ventures.

3.1 Understanding E-Commerce Business Models

The e-commerce landscape offers a variety of business models, each with its own advantages and challenges. This section provides an in-depth look at popular models, including dropshipping, wholesale, and private label, helping readers determine which is best suited to their goals and resources.

3.1.1 Dropshipping, Wholesale, and Private Label

Each e-commerce business model offers distinct benefits and operational requirements. Understanding the core features of these models is essential for making informed decisions.

1. **Dropshipping: Low Investment, High Flexibility**
   Dropshipping has become one of the most accessible e-commerce models, allowing entrepreneurs to sell products without holding inventory. Products are shipped directly from suppliers to customers, minimising upfront costs.

- **How Dropshipping Works**: The seller lists products on an online store, and when a customer places an order, the supplier fulfils it. Platforms like Shopify and Oberlo simplify this process.

- **Advantages of Dropshipping**: This model requires minimal initial investment, making it attractive for first-time entrepreneurs. Its scalability allows businesses to expand quickly without the need for warehousing.

- **Challenges of Dropshipping**: Profit margins can be lower due to supplier fees. Additionally, reliance on third-party suppliers can lead to quality control and shipping issues.

2. **Wholesale: Bulk Purchasing for Better Margins**
   In the wholesale model, businesses purchase products in bulk at a discounted rate and resell them to customers at a markup. This approach offers higher profit margins compared to dropshipping but requires upfront capital for inventory.

   - **How Wholesale Works**: Businesses source products from wholesalers and store them in a warehouse or fulfilment centre. They manage inventory and ship orders directly to customers.

   - **Advantages of Wholesale**: Buying in bulk reduces the cost per unit, increasing profit margins. Businesses have greater control over quality and inventory.

   - **Challenges of Wholesale**: Initial investment in inventory and storage space can be significant. Overestimating demand may lead to unsold stock and financial losses.

3. **Private Label: Building a Brand from Scratch**
   Private labelling involves creating a unique product under your brand name, typically by partnering with

manufacturers. This model requires higher investment but offers the potential for significant long-term growth.

- o **How Private Labelling Works**: Entrepreneurs work with manufacturers to produce customised products with their branding. These products are then sold through online stores or marketplaces.

- o **Advantages of Private Labelling**: Branding enhances perceived value, allowing for higher price points. Unique products face less direct competition compared to generic items.

- o **Challenges of Private Labelling**: High upfront costs for product development, manufacturing, and branding. Building brand recognition and trust can take time and marketing resources.

3.1.2 Choosing the Right Model for You

Selecting the most suitable e-commerce model depends on factors like budget, time commitment, and business goals. This subsection provides a framework to help readers identify the best fit for their circumstances.

1. **Evaluating Your Resources and Goals**
   The right e-commerce model aligns with your available resources and long-term vision. Consider financial capacity, time investment, and skill set when making your choice.

   - o **Budget Considerations**: Dropshipping is ideal for those with limited funds, while wholesale and private labelling require higher upfront investment.

   - o **Time Commitment**: Dropshipping requires less day-to-day involvement in logistics, making it suitable for part-time entrepreneurs. Private labelling demands more time for product development and marketing.

o **Skills and Experience**: Previous experience in marketing or supply chain management may influence the choice. For instance, private labelling benefits from branding and marketing expertise.

2. **Assessing Market Demand and Competition**
Understanding market trends and analysing competitors can guide your decision. Tools like Google Trends, Jungle Scout, and SEMrush help evaluate demand and competition levels.

o **Identifying Popular Niches**: Research niches with steady demand in the USA, UK, and European markets, such as sustainable products or home fitness equipment.

o **Evaluating Competition**: Entering a highly competitive niche like electronics may require unique selling points to stand out.

o **Testing Viability with Dropshipping**: For uncertain markets, dropshipping allows low-risk testing before committing to larger investments.

3. **Aligning with Personal Interests and Expertise**
Choosing a model that aligns with your passions and expertise increases the likelihood of long-term success. Passion-driven businesses often foster greater commitment and creativity.

o **Leveraging Existing Knowledge**: Experience in a specific industry can provide a competitive edge, such as leveraging fashion expertise for a private label clothing brand.

o **Focusing on Personal Interests**: Selling products you are passionate about, such as eco-friendly items, can enhance motivation and marketing authenticity.

- o **Avoiding Common Pitfalls**: Ensuring that your passion aligns with market demand helps avoid creating a product with limited appeal.

3.1.3 Managing Logistics and Fulfilment

Efficient logistics and fulfilment are critical to e-commerce success, regardless of the chosen model. This subsection explores strategies for streamlining operations, from supplier relationships to shipping solutions.

1. **Establishing Strong Supplier Relationships**
   Reliable suppliers ensure consistent product quality and on-time delivery. Building strong partnerships reduces risks and enhances customer satisfaction.

   - o **Researching and Vetting Suppliers**: Use platforms like Alibaba for private labelling or AliExpress for dropshipping to find reputable suppliers.

   - o **Negotiating Favourable Terms**: Discuss minimum order quantities (MOQs), payment terms, and return policies to secure advantageous agreements.

   - o **Monitoring Supplier Performance**: Regularly evaluate suppliers based on delivery times, defect rates, and responsiveness.

2. **Choosing Fulfilment Methods**
   Different fulfilment methods, from self-fulfilment to third-party logistics (3PL) providers, offer varying levels of control and scalability.

   - o **Self-Fulfilment for Small-Scale Operations**: Packing and shipping orders manually is cost-effective for new businesses with low order volumes.

- **Using 3PL Providers for Scalability**: Partnering with companies like ShipBob or Amazon FBA streamlines logistics, enabling businesses to focus on growth.

- **Hybrid Models for Flexibility**: Combining self-fulfilment with 3PL providers offers flexibility during peak seasons or business transitions.

3. **Streamlining Shipping and Returns**
   Fast, reliable shipping and hassle-free returns build customer trust and loyalty. Optimising these processes reduces costs and enhances the overall shopping experience.

   - **Offering Multiple Shipping Options**: Provide standard, expedited, and international shipping to accommodate diverse customer needs.

   - **Negotiating Shipping Rates**: Partner with couriers like UPS or FedEx to secure discounted rates, especially for high-volume shipments.

   - **Implementing a Clear Return Policy**: A transparent, customer-friendly return policy increases confidence in your brand, particularly in markets like the UK and Europe, where consumer rights are prioritised.

Conclusion

Understanding e-commerce business models is the foundation for building a successful online business. By evaluating options like dropshipping, wholesale, and private labelling, selecting the right model, and mastering logistics and fulfilment, entrepreneurs can create profitable, scalable operations. Success in e-commerce requires adaptability, market awareness, and a commitment to providing exceptional customer experiences.

In the next section, we will explore **Setting Up Your E-Commerce Store**, covering platform selection, website optimisation, and essential tools for attracting and retaining customers.

3.2 Setting Up Your E-Commerce Store

A well-designed and functional online store is the cornerstone of any successful e-commerce business. This section provides actionable steps for choosing the right e-commerce platform, customising the storefront for optimal user experience, and integrating tools to improve performance and streamline operations.

3.2.1 Choosing the Right E-Commerce Platform

Selecting the right platform is critical to your store's success. Factors like ease of use, scalability, and built-in features should align with your business goals and technical expertise.

1. **Comparing Popular Platforms: Shopify, WooCommerce, and BigCommerce**
   Each platform offers distinct advantages tailored to different needs, budgets, and markets.

   o **Shopify for Simplicity and Scalability**: Shopify is a user-friendly, all-in-one solution ideal for beginners. Its scalability makes it suitable for businesses targeting global markets, including the USA and Europe.

- **Key Features**: Customisable themes, built-in payment processing, and app integrations.

- **Costs and Pricing**: Monthly subscription fees with optional premium apps.

- **Global Reach**: Multi-language and multi-currency support.

o **WooCommerce for Flexibility**: As a WordPress plugin, WooCommerce offers unparalleled customisation options, making it ideal for tech-savvy entrepreneurs.

- **Key Features**: Open-source platform, free core features, and endless customisation.

- **Costs and Hosting**: Requires a hosting plan, domain, and potentially paid plugins.

- **Best For**: Businesses with specific design needs or existing WordPress sites.

o **BigCommerce for Larger Operations**: BigCommerce is a robust platform for scaling businesses, with advanced features designed for high-volume sellers.

- **Key Features**: Built-in SEO tools, multi-channel selling, and extensive analytics.

- **Costs and Fees**: Higher subscription costs, but no transaction fees.

- **Ideal Niches**: Businesses in electronics, fashion, or other competitive industries.

2. **Evaluating Platform Features for Your Needs**
   Different businesses require different platform capabilities, from payment processing to marketing tools.

   o **Payment Gateway Options**: Ensure the platform supports popular gateways like PayPal, Stripe, and Apple Pay to accommodate diverse customer preferences.

   o **Multi-Channel Integration**: Platforms that integrate with marketplaces like Amazon, eBay, and social media enhance reach and sales.

   o **Mobile Responsiveness**: With a significant percentage of global traffic coming from mobile devices, responsive design is non-negotiable.

3. **Adapting to Regional Preferences**
   Certain platforms perform better in specific regions due to localised features and support.

   o **Europe and the UK**: Platforms offering compliance with GDPR and VAT management tools are essential.

   o **USA**: Platforms with built-in tax calculation and shipping integrations cater well to large, domestic markets.

   o **Global Markets**: Platforms with multi-currency support and international shipping integrations are ideal for global sellers.

3.2.2 Designing and Customising Your Storefront

A visually appealing and user-friendly storefront builds trust and encourages purchases. Customisation should focus on aesthetics, navigation, and branding.

1. **Creating a Memorable Brand Identity**
   Your brand is the foundation of customer trust and loyalty. Consistent branding across your store builds recognition and credibility.

   - **Designing a Logo and Visuals**: Tools like Canva or Adobe Illustrator help create professional logos and graphics.

   - **Choosing a Colour Palette**: Colours evoke emotions; choose shades that resonate with your target audience. For example, green is often associated with sustainability.

   - **Crafting a Unique Value Proposition (UVP)**: A compelling UVP highlights what sets your store apart, such as eco-friendly products or fast shipping.

2. **Enhancing User Experience (UX) and Navigation**
   A seamless browsing experience increases the likelihood of conversions.

   - **Streamlining Navigation**: Use clear categories, filters, and search functions to make product discovery easy.

   - **Optimising Page Load Times**: Tools like Google PageSpeed Insights help identify and resolve loading issues.

   - **Providing Intuitive Checkout Options**: Offer guest checkout and multiple payment methods to reduce friction.

3. **Incorporating Essential Pages and Features**
   Key pages and features instil trust and provide necessary information to customers.

   o **About and Contact Pages**: Personalising these pages with brand stories and support options fosters trust.

   o **FAQ and Returns Policies**: Address common concerns to reduce hesitation.

   o **Product Pages with Detailed Descriptions**: Include high-quality images, specs, and reviews to increase conversions.

3.2.3 Integrating Tools and Technologies

The right tools can enhance efficiency, improve marketing, and provide insights into store performance. This subsection explores essential integrations for success.

1. **Analytics and Performance Tracking**
   Understanding customer behaviour and store performance helps refine strategies.

   o **Google Analytics Integration**: Track traffic sources, customer demographics, and sales conversions.

   o **Heatmaps and Session Recordings**: Tools like Hotjar reveal user interactions and areas for improvement.

   o **E-Commerce Dashboards**: Platforms like Shopify offer built-in dashboards for tracking key metrics.

2. **Marketing and Automation Tools**
   Automating marketing efforts saves time and ensures consistent engagement.

- o **Email Marketing Platforms**: Tools like Klaviyo or Mailchimp allow personalised campaigns and abandoned cart recovery.

- o **Social Media Scheduling**: Apps like Buffer or Hootsuite streamline posting across multiple platforms.

- o **Chatbots and Live Support**: AI-driven chatbots enhance customer service and boost conversions.

3. **Inventory Management and Logistics Software**
Efficient inventory management ensures smooth operations and prevents stockouts.

- o **Stock Tracking Tools**: Solutions like TradeGecko help monitor inventory in real time.

- o **Shipping Label Generators**: Software like ShipStation simplifies labelling and tracking for global shipments.

- o **Integrating Fulfilment Services**: Tools that sync with Amazon FBA or third-party warehouses reduce manual errors.

Conclusion

Setting up an e-commerce store involves selecting the right platform, designing an attractive storefront, and integrating tools to improve efficiency and customer experience. By focusing on these elements, entrepreneurs can create a solid foundation for their online business, ensuring scalability and sustainability.

In the next section, we will delve into **Marketing Strategies for E-Commerce Success**, providing actionable insights into SEO, paid advertising, and social media marketing to drive traffic and conversions.

3.3 Marketing Strategies for E-Commerce Success

Marketing is the lifeblood of e-commerce, turning a well-designed store into a profitable venture. This section covers essential strategies, including search engine optimisation (SEO), paid advertising, and social media marketing, to attract and convert customers effectively.

3.3.1 Search Engine Optimisation (SEO)

SEO is a cornerstone of e-commerce marketing, ensuring that your store ranks highly on search engines like Google. By optimising for relevant keywords and improving site performance, businesses can attract organic traffic and build long-term visibility.

1. **Keyword Research and Implementation**
   Identifying and targeting the right keywords ensures your store appears in search results for queries related to your products.

   o **Using SEO Tools for Research**: Platforms like Ahrefs, SEMrush, and Google Keyword Planner help identify high-traffic keywords in your niche.

     ▪ **Long-Tail Keywords**: Phrases like "sustainable yoga mats in the UK" target specific audiences with purchase intent.

     ▪ **Competitor Analysis**: Reviewing competitors' keywords provides insights into untapped opportunities.

   o **Integrating Keywords Strategically**: Incorporate keywords naturally into product titles, descriptions, and blog content to improve relevance.

- o **Local SEO for Regional Markets**: For businesses targeting specific regions, optimise content with location-based keywords, such as "affordable tech gadgets in Europe."

2. **Optimising On-Page and Technical SEO**
   On-page and technical SEO improvements enhance user experience and search engine rankings.

   - o **Improving Meta Tags and Descriptions**: Create compelling meta titles and descriptions for all product pages to increase click-through rates.

   - o **Enhancing Mobile Responsiveness**: With a growing percentage of traffic coming from mobile devices, a mobile-friendly design is critical.

   - o **Boosting Site Speed**: Tools like GTmetrix and Google PageSpeed Insights can help identify and fix speed issues.

3. **Building Backlinks and Content Marketing**
   Backlinks from reputable sources signal authority to search engines, while valuable content keeps visitors engaged.

   - o **Guest Blogging for Backlinks**: Writing for niche blogs can drive referral traffic and improve domain authority.

   - o **Creating Engaging Blog Content**: Blogs covering trends, product comparisons, or how-to guides position your store as a trusted resource.

   - o **Partnering with Influencers**: Influencer collaborations can generate backlinks and traffic, especially for lifestyle or fashion niches.

3.3.2 Paid Advertising

Paid ads can deliver immediate traffic and conversions, making them an essential part of a comprehensive e-commerce marketing strategy. This subsection explores effective use of platforms like Google Ads, Facebook Ads, and more.

1. **Google Ads for Search Visibility**
   Google Ads places your store in front of users searching for specific products, offering a high-intent audience.

   o **Running Search Campaigns**: Target keywords related to your products, such as "best hiking boots in Europe," to attract ready-to-buy customers.

   o **Leveraging Google Shopping**: Showcase product images, prices, and reviews directly in search results for higher engagement.

   o **Geo-Targeting for Regional Ads**: Focus on high-conversion regions, tailoring campaigns for specific markets like the USA or UK.

2. **Social Media Ads for Engagement and Sales**
   Platforms like Facebook, Instagram, and TikTok offer highly targeted ad solutions for reaching diverse audiences.

   o **Creating Visual Ad Campaigns**: Eye-catching visuals and videos perform well on Instagram and TikTok, especially for fashion or beauty products.

   o **Targeting by Demographics and Interests**: Facebook Ads Manager allows precise targeting, such as age, location, or interests, to maximise ROI.

   o **Retargeting for Abandoned Carts**: Use retargeting ads to re-engage visitors who left without completing a purchase.

3. **Budgeting and Tracking Ad Performance**
   Effective budget allocation and performance tracking ensure profitability from ad campaigns.

   o **Setting a Cost-Per-Acquisition (CPA) Goal**: Define acceptable costs for acquiring a customer based on average order value and profit margins.

   o **Using Analytics for Optimisation**: Platforms like Google Analytics and Facebook Ads Manager provide insights to refine campaigns.

   o **A/B Testing Ad Creatives**: Experiment with different headlines, visuals, and offers to identify what resonates best with your audience.

3.3.3 Social Media Marketing

Social media platforms are invaluable for building brand awareness, engaging with customers, and driving traffic to your store. This subsection outlines strategies for creating compelling content and leveraging platforms effectively.

1. **Building an Engaging Presence**
   Consistency and authenticity are key to fostering a loyal following on social media.

   o **Posting Regularly with a Content Calendar**: Plan and schedule posts to maintain an active presence.

   o **Showcasing User-Generated Content (UGC)**: Share photos or reviews from happy customers to build trust and authenticity.

   o **Using Stories and Reels for Immediate Engagement**: Short-form content on Instagram and TikTok keeps your brand top of mind.

2. **Running Contests and Giveaways**
   Contests and giveaways are effective for boosting engagement and growing your follower base.

- o **Creating Shareable Campaigns**: Encourage participants to tag friends or share posts to increase reach.

- o **Offering Relevant Prizes**: Ensure the giveaway aligns with your products to attract potential customers.

- o **Tracking Engagement Metrics**: Use platform analytics to measure the success of campaigns.

3. **Leveraging Influencer Marketing**
   Partnering with influencers can amplify your reach and build credibility.

   - o **Choosing the Right Influencers**: Micro-influencers often have higher engagement rates and more targeted audiences.

   - o **Collaborating on Sponsored Posts**: Work with influencers to create authentic content that showcases your products.

   - o **Measuring ROI**: Track traffic and sales generated from influencer campaigns to evaluate effectiveness.

Conclusion

A successful marketing strategy combines SEO, paid advertising, and social media marketing to drive traffic and conversions. By leveraging these techniques, e-commerce businesses can build visibility, foster engagement, and generate sales across global markets.

The next section will focus on **Scaling Your E-Commerce Business**, offering strategies for automation, international expansion, and data-driven decision-making to ensure sustainable growth.

3.4 Scaling Your E-Commerce Business

Once your e-commerce store is up and running, the next challenge is scaling operations to increase revenue and expand market reach. Scaling involves optimising workflows, entering new markets, and using data-driven strategies to make informed decisions. This section explores how to grow your business sustainably while maintaining efficiency and customer satisfaction.

3.4.1 Automation and Workflow Optimisation

Automating repetitive tasks and streamlining workflows saves time, reduces errors, and allows businesses to focus on growth strategies. This subsection provides actionable steps to optimise operations.

1. **Automating Order Management and Inventory**
   Automation tools simplify order processing, inventory tracking, and fulfilment, ensuring smoother operations as order volumes grow.

   - **Order Management Systems (OMS)**: Tools like TradeGecko or Zoho Inventory automate order processing, reducing manual errors.

   - **Real-Time Inventory Syncing**: Integrating inventory management tools with your store ensures accurate stock levels, preventing overselling.

   - **Streamlining Dropshipping Fulfilment**: Platforms like Oberlo or Modalyst automatically forward orders to suppliers, saving time and effort.

2. **Implementing Marketing Automation**
   Marketing automation tools enable consistent communication with customers, nurturing leads and boosting sales.

- o **Email Marketing Campaigns**: Tools like Klaviyo and Mailchimp automate personalised email sequences for abandoned carts, promotions, and customer follow-ups.

- o **Social Media Scheduling**: Apps like Buffer or Later streamline content posting across platforms, ensuring consistent engagement.

- o **Retargeting Campaigns**: Automated retargeting ads re-engage previous visitors, increasing conversion rates.

3. **Optimising Customer Support with AI**
   AI-powered tools enhance customer service, ensuring quick and efficient responses to inquiries.

   - o **Chatbots for 24/7 Support**: Chatbots like Zendesk or Tidio handle common queries and direct complex issues to human agents.

   - o **Knowledge Bases and FAQs**: Automating responses to frequently asked questions reduces the burden on support teams.

   - o **AI-Powered Analytics for Customer Insights**: Tools like HubSpot provide insights into customer behaviour, helping businesses tailor their support strategies.

3.4.2 Expanding into International Markets

International expansion is a powerful way to scale an e-commerce business, providing access to new customer bases and increasing revenue potential. This subsection outlines the steps to entering global markets successfully.

1. **Researching and Targeting New Markets**
   Expanding internationally requires a thorough understanding of regional preferences, regulations, and competition.

- o **Market Research Tools**: Use tools like Statista or NielsenIQ to gather insights on global trends and consumer behaviour.

- o **Identifying High-Potential Regions**: Focus on markets with strong demand for your products, such as sustainable goods in Europe or tech gadgets in the USA.

- o **Assessing Local Competition**: Analyse competitors' offerings and pricing strategies to identify gaps in the market.

2. **Adapting Your Store for Global Customers**
   Tailoring your e-commerce store to meet the needs of international customers improves user experience and increases conversions.

   - o **Multi-Language Support**: Translate your website into local languages using tools like Weglot or Bablic.

   - o **Currency Conversion**: Enable multi-currency pricing to simplify purchases for international customers.

   - o **Compliance with Regional Regulations**: Ensure GDPR compliance in Europe and account for sales tax or VAT requirements in the UK and USA.

3. **Managing International Shipping and Returns**
   Reliable shipping and clear return policies are critical to building trust with international customers.

   - o **Partnering with Global Couriers**: Collaborate with DHL, UPS, or FedEx to offer reliable and cost-effective shipping options.

   - o **Calculating Duties and Taxes**: Use platforms like Avalara or Easyship to calculate import duties and taxes for international orders.

- o **Simplifying Returns for Overseas Customers**: Provide pre-paid return labels and clear instructions to minimise friction in the return process.

3.4.3 Leveraging Data for Strategic Growth

Data analytics plays a crucial role in scaling e-commerce businesses by identifying opportunities, optimising performance, and predicting trends. This subsection explores how to use data effectively.

1. **Tracking Key Performance Indicators (KPIs)**
   Monitoring KPIs provides insights into business health and highlights areas for improvement.

   - o **Sales Metrics**: Analyse metrics like average order value (AOV), customer acquisition cost (CAC), and conversion rates.

   - o **Customer Retention Metrics**: Track repeat purchase rates and customer lifetime value (CLV) to assess loyalty.

   - o **Marketing Performance**: Measure return on ad spend (ROAS) and engagement rates across campaigns.

2. **Using Predictive Analytics for Demand Forecasting**
   Predictive analytics tools help anticipate customer behaviour, enabling better inventory and marketing decisions.

   - o **Demand Planning Software**: Tools like Forecastly or NetSuite use historical data to predict future demand, reducing overstock or stockouts.

   - o **Customer Segmentation**: Analyse customer behaviour to identify high-value segments and tailor marketing efforts accordingly.

- o **Seasonal Trends Analysis**: Identify peak seasons to prepare marketing campaigns and inventory ahead of time.

3. **A/B Testing for Continuous Optimisation**
Experimenting with different elements of your store and marketing campaigns ensures constant improvement.

- o **Testing Website Features**: A/B test homepage layouts, checkout processes, and calls-to-action (CTAs) to optimise user experience.

- o **Evaluating Marketing Campaigns**: Test variations of ad creatives, email subject lines, or promotional offers to find the most effective strategies.

- o **Leveraging Tools for Testing**: Platforms like Optimizely or Google Optimize simplify A/B testing and provide actionable insights.

Conclusion

Scaling an e-commerce business requires a combination of automation, international expansion, and data-driven decision-making. By streamlining workflows, entering new markets, and leveraging analytics, entrepreneurs can achieve sustainable growth while maintaining high levels of customer satisfaction.

The next section will explore **Building Customer Loyalty in E-Commerce**, focusing on strategies to foster repeat business, create brand advocates, and enhance the overall shopping experience.

3.5 Building Customer Loyalty in E-Commerce

Customer loyalty is critical for the long-term success of any e-commerce business. Loyal customers are more likely to make repeat purchases, refer others, and engage positively with your brand, making them invaluable to sustained growth. This section explores actionable strategies to foster loyalty, from personalised experiences to loyalty programmes and brand advocacy.

3.5.1 Creating a Personalised Customer Experience

Personalisation builds stronger connections between customers and your brand, fostering trust and repeat engagement. Tailoring every aspect of the customer journey enhances satisfaction and loyalty.

1. **Using Data to Understand Customer Preferences**
   Leveraging customer data enables businesses to create personalised experiences that resonate with individual preferences.

   - **Tracking Purchase History**: Analyse past purchases to recommend relevant products. For example, customers buying skincare items may appreciate recommendations for complementary products like moisturisers.

- o **Monitoring Browsing Behaviour**: Tools like Google Analytics track browsing habits, allowing for tailored product suggestions or targeted email campaigns.

- o **Segmenting Customers for Specific Messaging**: Grouping customers by demographics, behaviour, or location ensures targeted communication. For instance, promoting winter gear in colder regions of Europe during seasonal campaigns.

2. **Implementing Personalised Communication**
   Personalised communication builds trust and encourages engagement.

   - o **Email Personalisation**: Use customer names and tailor subject lines to highlight products they've shown interest in.

   - o **Dynamic Website Content**: Platforms like Shopify or Magento allow dynamic content that changes based on user preferences, such as showing region-specific promotions.

   - o **Automated Chat Suggestions**: Chatbots equipped with AI can recommend products or answer customer-specific queries based on prior interactions.

3. **Offering Tailored Discounts and Rewards**
   Specialised discounts make customers feel valued and increase the likelihood of repeat purchases.

   - o **Birthday Discounts**: Send personalised offers to customers during their birthday month.

   - o **First-Time Purchase Incentives**: Encourage repeat business by offering a discount on a customer's second purchase.

- o **Exclusive Offers for Loyal Customers**: Provide early access to sales or special discounts for frequent shoppers.

3.5.2 Developing Effective Loyalty Programmes

Loyalty programmes incentivise customers to return by offering tangible rewards for repeat purchases. A well-designed programme boosts customer retention and lifetime value.

1. **Choosing the Right Type of Loyalty Programme**
   Different loyalty programme models cater to varying customer preferences and business goals.

   - o **Point-Based Systems**: Customers earn points for every purchase, which can be redeemed for discounts or products. For example, every £1 spent earns 10 points, redeemable at 1,000 points.

   - o **Tiered Loyalty Levels**: Offer increasing benefits as customers progress through tiers, such as "Bronze," "Silver," and "Gold." Higher tiers could include perks like free shipping or priority customer service.

   - o **Subscription-Based Rewards**: Implement a paid membership model offering exclusive benefits, such as free next-day delivery or early access to sales.

2. **Integrating Loyalty Programmes with Technology**
   Streamlining programme management through technology ensures ease of use for both businesses and customers.

   - o **Loyalty Apps and Software**: Tools like Smile.io or Yotpo Loyalty provide easy-to-use interfaces for tracking rewards and engaging customers.

159

- o **Mobile Integration**: Allow customers to track points or access rewards via a mobile app.

- o **Automated Reward Distribution**: Automate reward allocation after purchases, ensuring seamless customer experience.

3. **Promoting Your Loyalty Programme**
   Clear communication is key to encouraging participation and maximising the programme's impact.

   - o **Highlighting Benefits on Your Website**: Create a dedicated loyalty page detailing the programme's perks and how to join.

   - o **Promoting on Social Media**: Use social platforms to showcase success stories or testimonials from existing programme members.

   - o **Incentivising Sign-Ups**: Offer a one-time bonus, like extra points or a discount, for joining the programme.

3.5.3 Turning Customers into Brand Advocates

Brand advocates are loyal customers who actively promote your business, often through word-of-mouth or social media. Building a strong advocacy network enhances credibility and attracts new customers.

1. **Encouraging Positive Reviews and Testimonials**
   Positive reviews and testimonials build trust with potential customers and boost brand reputation.

   - o **Requesting Reviews After Purchases**: Automate review requests via email or SMS a few days after delivery.

   - o **Incentivising Reviews**: Offer discounts or loyalty points for leaving reviews.

- o **Featuring Testimonials on Key Pages**: Highlight glowing reviews on your homepage, product pages, and social media.

2. **Launching Referral Programmes**
Referral programmes reward customers for recommending your store to friends and family.

- o **Designing Attractive Rewards**: Offer discounts or store credit to both the referrer and the referee. For instance, "Get £10 off your next purchase when a friend makes their first order."

- o **Using Referral Platforms**: Tools like ReferralCandy or PostAffiliatePro simplify tracking and managing referral rewards.

- o **Tracking ROI**: Measure the success of your programme by tracking new customer acquisitions and revenue generated through referrals.

3. **Engaging Customers Through Social Media**
Social media provides a platform for customers to share their experiences and advocate for your brand.

- o **Encouraging User-Generated Content (UGC)**: Run campaigns asking customers to share photos or videos using your products, tagged with a branded hashtag.

- o **Hosting Contests and Giveaways**: Reward customers for sharing your brand with their network. For example, a giveaway for the most creative photo featuring your product.

- o **Featuring Advocates in Marketing**: Highlight loyal customers or their content in your ads or social media posts to strengthen connections and encourage others to participate.

Conclusion

Building customer loyalty in e-commerce is about more than repeat purchases—it's about creating a positive, memorable experience that fosters trust and advocacy. By focusing on personalisation, loyalty programmes, and brand advocacy, businesses can cultivate a loyal customer base that drives sustained growth and profitability.

The next chapter will focus on **Cryptocurrency and Blockchain Opportunities**.

Chapter 4: Cryptocurrency and Blockchain Opportunities

The world of cryptocurrency and blockchain technology has emerged as a disruptive force in the global economy, reshaping how individuals and businesses think about finance, data security, and decentralisation. From offering new investment opportunities to enabling innovative applications across industries, cryptocurrencies and blockchain are creating pathways for financial empowerment and technological advancement.

In this chapter, we'll provide a foundational understanding of cryptocurrencies, their underlying blockchain technology, and the diverse opportunities they present. Whether you're looking to invest, build a blockchain-based business, or simply stay informed, this guide will help you navigate the evolving landscape with insights tailored to the USA, UK, European, and global markets.

Cryptocurrency: A Brief Overview

Cryptocurrencies are digital or virtual currencies that leverage cryptographic techniques to secure transactions and operate on decentralised networks. Unlike traditional money issued by governments, cryptocurrencies are built on blockchain technology, which ensures transparency, security, and independence from central authorities.

1. **A New Era of Digital Money**
   Cryptocurrencies have redefined the concept of money, introducing a decentralised financial system that allows peer-to-peer transactions without intermediaries like banks.

   o **Decentralisation**: In contrast to fiat currencies controlled by central banks, cryptocurrencies operate on distributed networks, making them resistant to censorship and manipulation.

- o **Borderless Transactions**: Cryptocurrencies enable fast, cost-effective cross-border transactions, providing an alternative to traditional banking systems.

- o **Transparency**: All transactions are recorded on an immutable public ledger, ensuring accountability and reducing fraud risks.

2. **The Growing Popularity of Cryptocurrencies**
Since Bitcoin's launch in 2009, cryptocurrencies have gained traction globally, with thousands of coins now available in the market.

- o **Investment Potential**: Cryptocurrencies like Bitcoin and Ethereum have seen significant price growth, attracting investors seeking high returns.

- o **Global Adoption**: Countries like El Salvador have adopted Bitcoin as legal tender, while others explore central bank digital currencies (CBDCs).

- o **Market Diversity**: Beyond Bitcoin, coins like Ethereum, Cardano, and Solana offer unique features and use cases, from smart contracts to decentralised apps (dApps).

3. **Challenges and Controversies**
Despite their potential, cryptocurrencies face scrutiny and challenges.

- o **Volatility**: Prices can fluctuate dramatically, posing risks for investors and users.

- o **Regulatory Uncertainty**: Governments worldwide are grappling with how to regulate cryptocurrencies without stifling innovation.

- o **Environmental Concerns**: Energy-intensive mining processes, particularly for Bitcoin, have raised concerns about sustainability.

4.1 Introduction to Cryptocurrency

Cryptocurrencies have transformed the financial world, offering new ways to transact, invest, and innovate. This section explores the fundamentals of cryptocurrency, its various types and applications, and the risks and rewards associated with this dynamic asset class. By understanding these aspects, readers can make informed decisions about engaging with cryptocurrencies in the USA, UK, European, and global markets.

4.1.1 What is Cryptocurrency and How It Works

Cryptocurrency is a digital or virtual form of currency that leverages cryptography for secure transactions and operates on decentralised networks, typically blockchain. Understanding how cryptocurrencies function is key to grasping their impact on the economy and their potential as financial tools.

1. **The Concept of Cryptocurrency**
    Cryptocurrencies are designed as an alternative to traditional fiat currencies, offering a decentralised and digital-first approach to money.

    o   **Decentralisation**: Unlike centralised banking systems, cryptocurrencies operate on distributed networks, eliminating intermediaries like banks.

    o   **Digital Nature**: Cryptocurrencies exist entirely online, stored in digital wallets and transacted via secure systems.

    o   **Blockchain Backbone**: Most cryptocurrencies rely on blockchain technology, a decentralised ledger that records all transactions transparently and immutably.

2. **How Cryptocurrency Transactions Work**

   The mechanics of cryptocurrency transactions set them apart from traditional payment systems.

   - **Blockchain Technology**: Transactions are validated by network participants (miners or validators) and recorded on a public ledger.

   - **Peer-to-Peer Transactions**: Cryptocurrencies enable direct exchanges between parties without requiring third-party approval.

   - **Public and Private Keys**: Wallets use cryptographic keys; public keys serve as addresses, while private keys enable access and control over funds.

3. **Cryptographic Security and Innovation**

   The use of cryptography ensures transaction security and underpins the unique features of cryptocurrencies.

   - **Encryption Standards**: Cryptographic techniques like SHA-256 provide robust security against tampering or fraud.

   - **Consensus Mechanisms**: Proof-of-Work (PoW) and Proof-of-Stake (PoS) are examples of consensus protocols that validate transactions and secure networks.

   - **Immutable Records**: The decentralised ledger structure prevents unauthorised changes, ensuring trust and transparency.

4.1.2 Types of Cryptocurrencies and Their Uses

Not all cryptocurrencies are created equal; they vary significantly in terms of purpose, technology, and application. This subsection categorises cryptocurrencies and highlights their unique features and roles in the financial ecosystem.

1. **Bitcoin: The Pioneer of Digital Currency**
   Bitcoin (BTC) was the first cryptocurrency, introducing blockchain technology and decentralisation to the world.

   o **Origin and Significance**: Created in 2009 by an anonymous figure known as Satoshi Nakamoto, Bitcoin set the foundation for all other cryptocurrencies.

   o **Store of Value**: Often referred to as digital gold, Bitcoin is primarily seen as a store of value and an inflation hedge.

   o **Global Adoption**: Bitcoin's acceptance as a payment method is growing in the USA, UK, and Europe, with companies like Tesla and Shopify enabling crypto transactions.

2. **Altcoins: Beyond Bitcoin**
   Altcoins refer to all cryptocurrencies other than Bitcoin, offering diverse functionalities and innovations.

   o **Ethereum (ETH)**: Known for its smart contract capabilities, Ethereum is a platform for decentralised applications (dApps) and NFTs.

   o **Ripple (XRP)**: Focused on cross-border payments, Ripple aims to facilitate fast and low-cost international transactions.

   o **Stablecoins (USDT, USDC)**: Pegged to traditional assets like USD or gold, stablecoins minimise volatility, making them ideal for daily transactions and remittances.

3. **Niche Cryptocurrencies and Emerging Trends**
   Specialised cryptocurrencies cater to specific industries or communities.

   o **DeFi Tokens**: Cryptocurrencies like Uniswap (UNI) and Aave (AAVE) power decentralised finance platforms, enabling lending, borrowing, and staking.

   o **Gaming and Metaverse Tokens**: Coins like Axie Infinity (AXS) and Decentraland (MANA) are central to blockchain-based gaming ecosystems.

   o **Privacy Coins**: Cryptocurrencies such as Monero (XMR) and Zcash (ZEC) prioritise anonymity and transaction privacy.

4.1.3 Risks and Rewards of Investing in Crypto

Cryptocurrencies offer significant opportunities for profit, but they also come with inherent risks. This subsection explores the balance of potential gains and challenges investors face in the crypto space.

---

1. **The Rewards of Cryptocurrency Investment**
   Cryptocurrencies have gained attention for their potential to deliver high returns and revolutionise traditional finance.

   o **High Returns on Investment**: Early adopters of Bitcoin, Ethereum, and other successful cryptocurrencies have seen exponential growth in their investments.

   o **Portfolio Diversification**: Adding crypto to investment portfolios offers exposure to a high-growth asset class uncorrelated with traditional markets.

o **Empowerment and Accessibility**:
Cryptocurrencies democratise finance, enabling
anyone with internet access to participate in
global markets.

2. **The Risks Involved in Crypto Investing**
Despite the potential rewards, cryptocurrencies are a
volatile and high-risk investment class.

o **Market Volatility**: The value of
cryptocurrencies can fluctuate drastically, often
influenced by speculation and market sentiment.

o **Regulatory Uncertainty**: Policies and
regulations vary across regions, with some
governments banning or restricting crypto usage.

o **Security Concerns**: Hacking, phishing, and
other cyberattacks can result in the loss of funds,
especially for users unfamiliar with securing
digital wallets.

3. **Strategies to Mitigate Risks**
Proper research, diversification, and risk management
can help minimise exposure to crypto-related risks.

o **DYOR (Do Your Own Research)**:
Understanding the technology, team, and use
case behind a cryptocurrency is essential before
investing.

o **Secure Storage Solutions**: Use hardware
wallets or multi-signature wallets to safeguard
assets.

o **Long-Term Perspective**: Treating
cryptocurrency as a long-term investment
reduces the impact of short-term market
fluctuations.

Conclusion

Cryptocurrency represents both an exciting innovation and a complex financial asset. By understanding how cryptocurrencies work, exploring their diverse applications, and weighing the risks and rewards of investing, individuals can make informed decisions about engaging with this transformative technology. As global adoption increases, cryptocurrencies are poised to play a significant role in shaping the future of finance.

The next section will delve deeper into **Blockchain Technology**, explaining its principles, applications, and transformative potential beyond cryptocurrencies.

4.2 Blockchain Beyond Cryptocurrency

Blockchain technology, often associated with cryptocurrencies, offers applications far beyond the financial realm. Its decentralised, transparent, and secure nature has the potential to transform industries, improve operational efficiencies, and bolster digital security. This section delves into the core principles of blockchain, its diverse use cases, and its role in safeguarding digital assets.

4.2.1 Understanding Blockchain Technology

Blockchain is a distributed ledger technology that underpins cryptocurrencies and other applications. To appreciate its potential, one must first understand its components, processes, and advantages.

1. **The Fundamentals of Blockchain**
    Blockchain operates as a decentralised database maintained across a network of computers (nodes), ensuring transparency and immutability.

    o   **Distributed Ledger**: Transactions are recorded in blocks, linked chronologically, and stored across multiple nodes, reducing centralised control.

- o **Consensus Mechanisms**: These protocols, such as Proof-of-Work (PoW) and Proof-of-Stake (PoS), validate transactions and maintain ledger integrity.

- o **Immutability**: Once a block is added, its data cannot be altered without consensus, ensuring tamper-proof records.

2. **Blockchain Architecture**

The architecture of a blockchain system defines how it operates and interacts with its environment.

- o **Public vs. Private Blockchains**: Public blockchains like Ethereum are accessible to anyone, while private blockchains are restricted to specific participants, often used in corporate settings.

- o **Smart Contracts**: Self-executing contracts with terms encoded into the blockchain automate processes and reduce reliance on intermediaries.

- o **Sidechains and Layer 2 Solutions**: Secondary frameworks like Polygon enhance scalability and efficiency while interacting with primary blockchains.

3. **Advantages of Blockchain**

Blockchain's unique attributes make it a revolutionary technology across various fields.

- o **Transparency**: All participants in the network can view transaction history, fostering trust and accountability.

- o **Decentralisation**: Reduces dependency on central authorities, mitigating risks associated with single points of failure.

- o **Security**: Cryptographic hashing and consensus protocols make blockchain highly resistant to fraud and cyberattacks.

4.2.2 Potential Use Cases in Various Industries

Blockchain's versatility enables its application across numerous sectors, streamlining processes and fostering innovation. This subsection highlights key industries benefiting from blockchain.

1. **Finance and Banking**
   Beyond powering cryptocurrencies, blockchain revolutionises traditional financial systems by improving efficiency and security.

   - o **Cross-Border Payments**: Blockchain eliminates intermediaries, reducing costs and speeding up transactions, especially for remittances in regions like Europe and Southeast Asia.

   - o **Decentralised Finance (DeFi)**: Platforms like Uniswap and Compound enable lending, borrowing, and trading without traditional banks, increasing financial inclusion.

   - o **Fraud Prevention**: Blockchain's transparency and immutability reduce fraudulent activities in banking and credit systems.

2. **Supply Chain and Logistics**
   Blockchain enhances traceability, transparency, and efficiency in supply chains, addressing long-standing challenges.

   - o **Tracking Provenance**: Consumers in the UK and USA increasingly demand transparency in product sourcing, which blockchain can provide for goods like coffee and diamonds.

o **Reducing Fraud and Counterfeiting**: Immutable records validate the authenticity of products, particularly in pharmaceuticals and luxury goods.

o **Improving Efficiency**: Smart contracts automate processes like inventory management and payment settlements.

3. **Healthcare**
Blockchain addresses critical challenges in healthcare, such as data security and interoperability.

o **Electronic Health Records (EHRs)**: Blockchain enables secure, patient-controlled health records, enhancing privacy and data sharing.

o **Drug Traceability**: Ensuring the authenticity of medications through blockchain reduces counterfeit drugs in Europe and Asia.

o **Clinical Trials and Research**: Transparent data sharing in trials fosters collaboration and accelerates breakthroughs.

4. **Energy and Sustainability**
Blockchain supports renewable energy adoption and environmental initiatives.

o **Energy Trading**: Platforms like Power Ledger enable peer-to-peer energy trading, making renewable energy accessible and affordable.

o **Carbon Credit Markets**: Blockchain tracks and verifies carbon credits, ensuring accountability in global sustainability efforts.

o **Resource Management**: Smart contracts optimise resource allocation and reduce waste in industries like agriculture.

4.2.3 The Role of Blockchain in Digital Security

Blockchain offers robust solutions to modern security challenges, protecting sensitive data and mitigating cyber threats. This subsection explores its critical role in enhancing digital security.

1. **Enhancing Data Integrity and Privacy**
   Blockchain safeguards data from unauthorised access and tampering, addressing key concerns in the digital era.

   o **Decentralised Data Storage**: Distributed networks reduce vulnerability to hacks compared to centralised servers.

   o **Encryption and Anonymity**: Cryptographic techniques protect user identities, balancing transparency with privacy.

   o **Data Verification**: Blockchain verifies the authenticity of information, crucial in combating misinformation and fake news.

2. **Securing Digital Identities**
   Digital identity solutions built on blockchain empower individuals while reducing fraud.

   o **Self-Sovereign Identity (SSI)**: Users control their digital identities without reliance on central authorities, enhancing privacy and reducing identity theft.

   o **Biometric Integration**: Combining blockchain with biometrics strengthens identity verification processes, particularly in finance and travel.

   o **Interoperability**: Blockchain enables seamless identity verification across platforms, simplifying user experiences globally.

3. **Combating Cybersecurity Threats**
   Blockchain's resilience to cyberattacks makes it a valuable asset in combating emerging threats.

   o **Ransomware Protection**: Immutable transaction records reduce the effectiveness of ransomware attacks.

   o **IoT Security**: Blockchain secures Internet of Things (IoT) devices by decentralising data management and ensuring device integrity.

   o **DDoS Attack Mitigation**: Distributed ledger systems mitigate the risk of Distributed Denial of Service (DDoS) attacks, enhancing network reliability.

Conclusion

Blockchain technology has far-reaching implications beyond cryptocurrency, offering transformative potential across industries and revolutionising digital security. Its decentralised and transparent nature makes it an invaluable tool for innovation and efficiency in the USA, UK, European, and global markets. As adoption grows, blockchain will continue to shape the future of finance, healthcare, supply chains, and beyond.

The next section will explore **Earning in the Crypto Space**, providing readers with strategies to identify opportunities and navigate challenges in this evolving space.

4.3 Earning Opportunities in the Crypto Space

The cryptocurrency industry offers a wide range of earning opportunities, from passive income generation to active participation in innovative projects. This section explores key methods for earning in the crypto space, including staking, mining, yield farming, investing in token launches, and freelancing with cryptocurrency payments. By understanding these opportunities, individuals can diversify income streams and navigate this dynamic market.

4.3.1 Staking, Mining, and Yield Farming

These methods of earning cryptocurrency rely on supporting blockchain networks or participating in decentralised finance (DeFi) protocols. Each approach offers varying levels of complexity, risk, and reward.

1. **Staking: Passive Income by Securing Networks**
   Staking involves locking up cryptocurrency to support the operations of a blockchain network, earning rewards in return.

   o **How Staking Works**: In Proof-of-Stake (PoS) systems, participants lock their coins in a wallet to validate transactions and maintain the blockchain.

   o **Rewards for Staking**: Stakers earn a percentage of transaction fees or newly minted coins, often yielding higher returns than traditional savings accounts.

   o **Popular Staking Platforms**: Networks like Ethereum (ETH), Cardano (ADA), and Polkadot (DOT) offer staking opportunities. Platforms such as Binance and Kraken simplify the process for retail investors.

Subsections for Staking:

   o **Selecting Coins for Staking**: Factors to consider, such as annual percentage yields (APYs), network stability, and market trends.

   o **Using Staking Pools**: For individuals with fewer coins, pooling resources increases the likelihood of earning rewards.

o **Risks of Staking**: Risks include network failure, token devaluation, and lock-in periods during which staked coins cannot be withdrawn.

2. **Mining: Earning by Validating Transactions**
   Mining, a key process in Proof-of-Work (PoW) systems like Bitcoin, rewards participants who solve complex algorithms to validate transactions.

   o **Setting Up Mining Operations**: Requirements include high-powered hardware (ASICs or GPUs), electricity, and software to join a mining pool.

   o **Mining Rewards**: Miners earn block rewards and transaction fees, with profitability depending on hardware efficiency and energy costs.

   o **Environmental Concerns**: Mining's energy consumption has drawn criticism, especially in Europe, where sustainability initiatives are prioritised.

Subsections for Mining:

   o **Solo vs. Pool Mining**: Comparing profitability and risk in independent mining versus collaborative pools.

   o **Legal and Tax Implications**: Navigating regulations and tax obligations for mining in the USA, UK, and other jurisdictions.

   o **Shifts to Green Mining**: Exploring renewable energy solutions and eco-friendly mining projects.

3. **Yield Farming: High-Risk, High-Reward Strategies**
   Yield farming involves lending or staking cryptocurrency in DeFi protocols to generate returns, often in the form of interest or additional tokens.

- o **How Yield Farming Works**: Users provide liquidity to decentralised exchanges (DEXs) or lending platforms, earning a share of transaction fees or governance tokens.

- o **Top Platforms for Yield Farming**: Platforms like Uniswap, PancakeSwap, and Aave offer lucrative farming opportunities.

- o **Risks and Volatility**: Impermanent loss, smart contract vulnerabilities, and volatile market conditions can erode gains.

Subsections for Yield Farming:

- o **Choosing the Right Pools**: Factors to assess, such as token pairs, APYs, and platform reputation.

- o **Managing Risks in Yield Farming**: Strategies to mitigate impermanent loss and diversify across pools.

- o **Regulatory Concerns**: How DeFi is evolving under regulatory scrutiny, particularly in the USA and Europe.

4.3.2 Participating in Initial Coin Offerings (ICOs) and Token Sales

ICOs and token sales provide early access to promising blockchain projects, often yielding substantial returns for successful investments. This subsection explores how to evaluate and participate in these opportunities.

1. **Understanding ICOs and Token Sales**
   ICOs allow blockchain projects to raise funds by selling tokens to early investors, while token sales distribute assets before they are widely traded.

- **Types of Token Sales**: Public ICOs, private sales, and Initial DEX Offerings (IDOs) on decentralised exchanges.

- **Investor Incentives**: Early access to discounted tokens and the potential for high returns as projects grow.

- **Risks and Scams**: Unregulated markets can attract fraudulent projects, making due diligence essential.

Subsections for Understanding ICOs:

- **The Evolution of ICOs**: From the early days of Ethereum's ICO to the rise of IDOs on platforms like Binance Launchpad.

- **Key Terminology**: Understanding whitepapers, tokenomics, and vesting schedules.

- **Differentiating Security Tokens vs. Utility Tokens**: Clarifying rights associated with each type of token.

2. **Evaluating ICOs for Potential Success**
   Thorough research and evaluation are critical when selecting ICOs to invest in.

   - **Project Fundamentals**: Assess the team, technology, and use case of the blockchain project.

   - **Market Position and Competitors**: Analyse the project's competitive advantage in the crypto ecosystem.

   - **Token Economics**: Study supply, distribution, and incentives for long-term growth.

Subsections for Evaluation:

- o **Red Flags in ICOs**: Common warning signs, such as vague whitepapers and unrealistic promises.

- o **Using ICO Rating Platforms**: Sites like ICObench and CoinMarketCap for informed decision-making.

- o **Legal Considerations**: Understanding regulatory requirements for ICOs in different regions, such as the USA's SEC guidelines.

3. **Participating in ICOs and Token Sales**
   The process of joining an ICO or token sale involves specific steps to ensure security and compliance.

   - o **Setting Up Wallets and Accounts**: Use secure wallets like MetaMask or Ledger to store tokens.

   - o **Navigating Whitelisting and KYC**: Most ICOs require identity verification and registration.

   - o **Avoiding Phishing Scams**: Best practices for safeguarding against fraudulent ICO websites and fake token addresses.

4.3.3 Freelancing and Getting Paid in Cryptocurrency

Cryptocurrency is increasingly accepted as a form of payment for freelance work, offering global opportunities and financial flexibility. This subsection outlines how to leverage crypto payments for freelancing success.

1. **Platforms Offering Crypto Payments**
   Several freelance platforms and marketplaces facilitate payments in cryptocurrency.

   - o **Dedicated Crypto Freelance Sites**: Platforms like CryptoTask and Bitwage allow freelancers to earn in Bitcoin and other cryptocurrencies.

- o **Traditional Platforms Adopting Crypto**: Upwork and Fiverr now support crypto payments for select transactions.

- o **Decentralised Marketplaces**: Blockchain-based platforms like Hive or Ethlance eliminate intermediaries, reducing fees.

Subsections for Crypto Payment Platforms:

- o **Benefits of Crypto Payments**: Faster transactions, lower fees, and accessibility for freelancers in underbanked regions.

- o **Selecting Reliable Platforms**: Key factors like security, user base, and supported cryptocurrencies.

- o **Legal and Tax Implications**: Reporting crypto earnings for tax purposes in the UK, USA, and Europe.

2. **Negotiating Crypto Payment Terms**
   Establishing clear terms ensures smooth transactions and avoids misunderstandings.

- o **Setting Conversion Rates**: Agree on exchange rates at the time of payment to avoid volatility disputes.

- o **Splitting Payments**: Combining crypto and fiat payments for flexibility.

- o **Drafting Contracts**: Use smart contracts to automate payments upon project completion.

Subsections for Payment Terms:

- o **Best Practices for Invoicing**: Clear itemisation and real-time updates on payment status.

- o **Handling Volatility**: Options for stablecoin payments to mitigate market fluctuations.

- o **Building Long-Term Client Relationships**: Transparency and professionalism in crypto payments foster trust.

3. **Building a Crypto-Based Freelance Career**
Earning in cryptocurrency opens unique opportunities for freelancers to expand their reach and income.

- o **Marketing Yourself in the Crypto Space**: Highlight blockchain-related skills and target crypto-savvy clients.

- o **Accepting International Clients**: Crypto eliminates cross-border payment issues, expanding global client bases.

- o **Investing Earnings in Crypto Projects**: Freelancers can reinvest earnings into staking or token sales for additional growth.

Conclusion

The crypto space offers diverse earning opportunities, from staking and mining to ICO investments and freelance work. Each method requires understanding, strategic planning, and risk management. By leveraging these opportunities, individuals in the USA, UK, Europe, and beyond can diversify income streams and take advantage of the growing blockchain economy.

In the next section, we will explore **Regulatory Frameworks and Legal Considerations in Cryptocurrency**, providing essential insights to navigate the evolving legal landscape.

4.4 Risks and Legal Considerations in Crypto

The cryptocurrency market offers exciting opportunities but comes with significant risks and regulatory complexities. Navigating these aspects is crucial for individuals and businesses looking to engage in the crypto space. This section covers the regulatory landscape, tips for avoiding scams and fraud, and tax implications to ensure compliance and safeguard investments.

4.4.1 Regulatory Landscape and Compliance

Cryptocurrency regulations vary across countries and regions, reflecting different approaches to balancing innovation and consumer protection. Understanding the evolving regulatory landscape is essential for compliance and long-term success.

1. **Global Variations in Cryptocurrency Regulation**
   Regulatory frameworks differ significantly worldwide, shaping how cryptocurrencies are used and traded.
   - **The USA's Approach**: The United States has a fragmented regulatory environment, with agencies like the SEC, CFTC, and IRS overseeing different aspects of the crypto market.
     - **Securities Classification**: The SEC regulates tokens considered securities, subjecting them to stringent requirements.
     - **Commodity Designation**: Cryptocurrencies like Bitcoin are treated as commodities, falling under CFTC jurisdiction.
     - **State-Level Regulations**: States like New York have specific licensing requirements, such as the BitLicense.
   - **UK's Regulatory Framework**: The Financial Conduct Authority (FCA) oversees cryptocurrency activities, focusing on anti-money laundering (AML) and consumer protection.

- **AML and KYC Requirements**: Exchanges must comply with Know Your Customer (KYC) and AML standards to operate in the UK.

- **Advertising Restrictions**: The FCA regulates crypto-related marketing to ensure transparency and accuracy.

- **Stablecoin Regulations**: The UK is exploring frameworks to regulate stablecoins as a means of payment.

  o **European Union Directives**: The EU employs a harmonised approach through regulations like the Markets in Crypto-Assets (MiCA) framework.

    - **MiCA Framework**: Establishes uniform rules for issuing and trading crypto-assets across member states.

    - **Privacy and Data Protection**: Compliance with GDPR is essential for crypto projects handling user data.

    - **Taxonomies and Definitions**: The EU classifies tokens into categories such as utility tokens and security tokens.

2. **Key Regulatory Challenges for Crypto Businesses**
   Navigating the regulatory environment requires careful consideration of compliance and operational risks.

   o **Licensing Requirements**: Obtaining licences in different jurisdictions can be complex and resource-intensive.

   o **Cross-Border Transactions**: Varying rules across regions create challenges for international crypto operations.

- o **Legal Uncertainty**: Rapidly evolving regulations mean businesses must stay updated to avoid penalties.

3. **Compliance Strategies for Individuals and Businesses**
   Proactive measures can ensure adherence to regulations while fostering trust among stakeholders.

   - o **Legal Consultation**: Engaging legal experts familiar with regional crypto laws minimises risks.

   - o **Implementing AML/KYC Protocols**: Robust compliance systems ensure transparency and regulatory alignment.

   - o **Monitoring Regulatory Updates**: Subscribing to updates from regulatory bodies helps businesses adapt swiftly to changes.

4.4.2 Avoiding Scams and Frauds

The crypto space, while promising, is rife with scams and fraudulent schemes targeting unsuspecting investors. Understanding how to identify and avoid these risks is critical for protecting assets.

1. **Common Types of Crypto Scams**
   Scammers employ various tactics to exploit the complexity and novelty of cryptocurrencies.

   - o **Phishing Attacks**: Fraudsters trick users into revealing private keys or wallet credentials through fake emails or websites.

   - o **Ponzi Schemes**: Promising high returns, these schemes collapse when new investments dry up, leaving earlier participants at a loss.

- o **Rug Pulls**: Developers abandon projects after collecting significant funds, often through decentralised finance (DeFi) platforms.

Subsections for Common Scams:

- o **Fake ICOs and Airdrops**: Scammers lure investors with false promises of exclusive tokens or projects.

- o **Imposter Profiles**: Fraudsters impersonate influencers or companies to solicit funds.

- o **Malware and Fake Apps**: Malicious software or apps compromise users' wallets and personal data.

2. **Red Flags to Watch For**
   Identifying warning signs can help users avoid falling victim to scams.

- o **Unrealistic Promises**: Offers of guaranteed returns with little risk are often too good to be true.

- o **Lack of Transparency**: Anonymous teams or vague project details signal potential fraud.

- o **High-Pressure Tactics**: Scammers often create urgency to push users into hasty decisions.

Subsections for Red Flags:

- o **Scrutinising Whitepapers**: Ensure project documentation is thorough and credible.

- o **Checking Smart Contract Code**: For DeFi projects, verifying open-source code can reveal vulnerabilities.

- o **Researching the Team and Backers**: Confirm the identities and reputations of project developers and investors.

3. **Steps to Protect Against Scams**
   Adopting safe practices and tools can safeguard investments and data.

   o **Using Reputable Exchanges**: Stick to well-established platforms like Coinbase, Binance, or Kraken.

   o **Enabling Two-Factor Authentication (2FA)**: Add an extra layer of security to wallets and accounts.

   o **Educating Yourself**: Staying informed about common scams and best practices is the first line of defence.

4.4.3 Tax Implications and Reporting

Taxation in the crypto space is complex and varies significantly by region. Ensuring accurate reporting and compliance with tax authorities is essential to avoid legal repercussions.

1. **Understanding Crypto Taxation**
   Most countries treat cryptocurrencies as taxable assets, subject to income, capital gains, or other taxes.

   o **Capital Gains Tax**: Applies to profits from selling or trading cryptocurrencies in the USA, UK, and EU.

   o **Income Tax**: Earnings from mining, staking, or freelancing in crypto are often classified as taxable income.

   o **VAT and Transaction Taxes**: Some regions, like the EU, apply VAT to certain crypto-related transactions.

Subsections for Taxation:

- o **Taxable Events**: Identifying events like selling, exchanging, or spending cryptocurrencies.

- o **Deductible Expenses**: Mining costs, transaction fees, and losses can often be deducted.

- o **Regional Differences**: Comparing tax treatments in the USA, UK, and Europe.

2. **Best Practices for Crypto Tax Reporting**
   Proper record-keeping and accurate reporting ensure compliance and minimise risks.

- o **Tracking Transactions**: Use tools like CoinTracking or CryptoTrader.Tax to monitor activity.

- o **Calculating Gains and Losses**: Understand methods like FIFO (First In, First Out) and LIFO (Last In, First Out) for cost basis calculation.

- o **Filing Taxes Correctly**: Follow local guidelines for submitting crypto-related income and gains.

Subsections for Reporting:

- o **Software Solutions**: Platforms like Koinly simplify crypto tax calculations and reporting.

- o **Common Errors to Avoid**: Misreporting income or failing to report transactions can trigger audits.

- o **Amnesty and Voluntary Disclosure**: Programmes in some countries allow individuals to correct past errors.

3. **Penalties for Non-Compliance**
   Failure to adhere to tax regulations can result in fines, audits, or legal action.

- o **Fines and Interest**: Penalties for late or inaccurate filings vary by region.

- o **Increased Scrutiny**: Non-compliance can attract closer examination from tax authorities.

- o **Legal Consequences**: Severe cases of tax evasion may lead to prosecution.

Conclusion

The crypto space offers immense potential but is fraught with risks and legal complexities. By understanding regulatory requirements, adopting robust security practices, and adhering to tax obligations, individuals and businesses can engage confidently in this evolving market. Navigating these challenges requires diligence, education, and a proactive approach to compliance.

The next chapter will explore **Freelancing and Remote Work Opportunities**, providing insights into what lies ahead for this transformative industry.

Chapter 5: Freelancing and Remote Work Opportunities

The global shift towards freelancing and remote work has transformed traditional employment models, offering individuals unprecedented flexibility and access to international markets. Advances in technology, the rise of digital platforms, and changing attitudes towards work-life balance have accelerated this trend, creating a thriving ecosystem of opportunities for freelancers and remote workers worldwide.

This chapter explores the foundations of freelancing and remote work, providing insights into the skills, tools, and platforms that enable individuals to succeed in this dynamic landscape. Whether you're based in the USA, the UK, Europe, or beyond, freelancing and remote work offer a gateway to financial independence, geographical freedom, and diversified income streams.

The Evolution of Freelancing and Remote Work

Freelancing and remote work have existed for decades, but the digital age has revolutionised how and where people work. Several key factors have contributed to this transformation:

1. **Technological Advancements**
   Innovations in communication and collaboration tools have made remote work seamless and efficient.

   o **Internet and Connectivity**: High-speed internet enables real-time communication and access to global clients, crucial in markets like the USA and Europe.

   o **Collaboration Software**: Platforms like Slack, Trello, and Zoom foster team productivity regardless of location.

   o **Secure Payment Gateways**: Services such as PayPal and Wise simplify international transactions, ensuring timely payments for freelancers.

2. **Shifts in Workforce Preferences**
   Workers across regions are increasingly prioritising flexibility, autonomy, and work-life balance.

   o **Remote-First Companies**: Businesses in the USA and UK are adopting remote-first policies, allowing employees to work from anywhere.

   o **Freelance Economy Growth**: According to a 2023 report, over 35% of the global workforce participates in freelancing, with significant contributions from Europe and Asia.

   o **Changing Attitudes Post-Pandemic**: COVID-19 normalised remote work, proving its feasibility across industries.

3. **Expansion of Digital Marketplaces**
   Online platforms have made it easier than ever to find freelance gigs or remote positions.

   o **Freelance Platforms**: Websites like Upwork, Fiverr, and Toptal connect skilled professionals with global clients.

   o **Industry-Specific Niches**: Platforms such as Dribbble (design) and ProBlogger (writing) cater to specialised talents.

   o **Corporate Adoption**: Major companies like Microsoft and Google are leveraging remote contractors for specialised projects.

Now let's get into more detail.

5.1 Setting Up a Freelancing Business

Starting a freelancing business provides the flexibility to work independently, earn a steady income, and engage with clients across global markets. However, success in freelancing requires strategic planning, leveraging the right platforms, and presenting yourself effectively to attract clients. This section provides a step-by-step guide to laying the foundation for a thriving freelancing career.

5.1.1 Choosing Your Niche and Skillset

Selecting the right niche and skillset is the cornerstone of a successful freelancing business. Focusing on your strengths and aligning them with market demand increases your chances of attracting high-value clients.

1. **Identifying Marketable Skills**
   Evaluate your abilities and determine which are most valuable to potential clients.

   - **Assessing Your Strengths**: Consider technical skills (e.g., graphic design, programming) and soft skills (e.g., communication, problem-solving).

   - **Matching Skills to Market Demand**: Research industries experiencing growth, such as content creation in the UK or software development in the USA.

   - **Developing In-Demand Skills**: Upskill through online courses or certifications in high-demand fields like digital marketing or data analysis.

2. **Researching Profitable Niches**
   A focused niche differentiates you from competitors and appeals to specific client needs.

- **Popular Niches**: Writing, graphic design, and IT services are evergreen niches with consistent demand.

- **Emerging Opportunities**: Explore new fields like NFT design, blockchain development, or AI-based solutions.

- **Regional Trends**: In Europe, sustainability consulting is growing, while remote bookkeeping is popular in the USA.

3. **Combining Passion with Profitability**
   Aligning personal interests with marketable skills fosters long-term motivation.

   - **Passion-Driven Projects**: Work in areas you're passionate about, such as social media management for non-profits.

   - **Evaluating Profit Margins**: Ensure your niche offers opportunities for high-paying clients or recurring income.

   - **Staying Adaptable**: Be open to evolving your niche as market trends shift or your expertise deepens.

5.1.2 Platforms for Freelancers (Upwork, Fiverr, etc.)

Freelancing platforms provide access to global clients and streamline the process of finding work. Choosing the right platform is critical to maximising your opportunities.

1. **Overview of Major Freelancing Platforms**
   Different platforms cater to varying industries and skill levels.

   - **Upwork**: Ideal for professionals offering a wide range of services, from writing to programming.

- **Fiverr**: Best suited for creatives and entry-level freelancers offering fixed-price gigs.

- **Toptal**: Targets experienced professionals in tech, finance, and design, with rigorous screening processes.

Subsections for Platform Overview:

- **Platform Fees**: Compare commission structures; Fiverr charges 20%, while Upwork tiers fees based on lifetime earnings.

- **User Demographics**: Evaluate platform-specific client bases, such as startups on Upwork or small businesses on PeoplePerHour.

- **Ease of Use**: Assess usability, from job discovery to payment withdrawal.

2. **Industry-Specific Platforms**
   Specialised platforms cater to niche professionals, offering targeted opportunities.

- **Design and Development**: Behance, Dribbble, and 99designs focus on visual creators and web developers.

- **Content and Writing**: ProBlogger and Contently are excellent for freelance writers and content strategists.

- **Consulting and Coaching**: Catalant and Clarity.fm connect experts with clients seeking strategic advice.

Subsections for Specialised Platforms:

- **Networking Potential**: Industry-specific platforms foster connections with peers and clients.

o **Platform-Specific Tools**: Features like Behance portfolios or ProBlogger job boards enhance visibility.

o **Client Quality**: Niche platforms often attract higher-paying, serious clients.

3. **Navigating Platform Policies and Guidelines**
   Understanding the rules of each platform ensures compliance and protects your reputation.

   o **Payment Policies**: Familiarise yourself with payment timelines and escrow features.

   o **Dispute Resolution**: Learn how to handle conflicts over deliverables or payments.

   o **Account Security**: Use two-factor authentication and avoid sharing sensitive information.

5.1.3 Crafting an Effective Profile and Portfolio

An impressive profile and portfolio are your most powerful tools for attracting clients. They showcase your skills, experience, and unique value proposition.

1. **Building a Professional Profile**
   A complete and compelling profile increases visibility and credibility on freelancing platforms.

   o **Headline and Summary**: Craft a concise, engaging headline and summary highlighting your expertise.

   o **Skills and Certifications**: List relevant abilities and credentials, such as Google Ads certification or Adobe Creative Cloud proficiency.

   o **Client Reviews and Ratings**: Display positive feedback from previous projects to build trust.

Subsections for Profile Building:

- o **Keyword Optimisation**: Use industry-relevant keywords to improve profile searchability.

- o **Profile Photos**: Upload a professional, approachable photo to personalise your profile.

- o **Customising for Platforms**: Tailor your profile to platform-specific preferences, like gig descriptions on Fiverr.

2. **Showcasing Your Work in a Portfolio**
   A well-organised portfolio demonstrates your capabilities and helps clients visualise the value you bring.

- o **Selecting Projects**: Include diverse examples that reflect your niche and showcase your best work.

- o **Presentation Tools**: Use platforms like Behance, LinkedIn, or your own website for portfolio hosting.

- o **Context and Results**: Provide brief case studies with metrics or client testimonials to highlight impact.

Subsections for Portfolio Development:

- ○ **Visual Portfolios**: For designers and photographers, focus on high-resolution visuals and layout design.

- ○ **Writing Samples**: Writers should feature a mix of blog posts, articles, and web copy to demonstrate versatility.

- ○ **Interactive Demos**: Developers can use GitHub or custom sites to showcase live project examples.

3. **Tailoring Applications and Proposals**
   Customising each proposal increases your chances of landing projects and impressing clients.

   - ○ **Researching Clients**: Understand client needs by reviewing their project descriptions and company background.

   - ○ **Highlighting Relevant Skills**: Focus on your unique qualifications that align with the client's objectives.

   - ○ **Offering Value Propositions**: Suggest solutions or additional services to exceed expectations.

Subsections for Proposal Crafting:

- ○ **Writing Attention-Grabbing Introductions**: Begin with personalised greetings and a clear understanding of the project.

- ○ **Avoiding Generic Pitches**: Stand out by addressing specific project challenges or goals.

- ○ **Following Up Professionally**: Send polite follow-ups to express continued interest in the opportunity.

Conclusion

Setting up a freelancing business requires thoughtful planning, from choosing the right niche to creating a standout portfolio. By leveraging the right platforms, understanding client needs, and presenting yourself effectively, freelancers can position themselves for success in competitive markets across the USA, UK, Europe, and beyond.

The next section will delve into **Maximising Income with Your Freelance Services**, providing actionable strategies for building a client base, expanding your reach, and growing your freelancing business sustainably.

5.2 Maximising Income as a Freelancer

Earning a sustainable and substantial income as a freelancer requires strategic planning, excellent client management, and a deep understanding of pricing dynamics. This section explores actionable methods to optimise your income, including setting effective pricing, attracting high-paying clients, and fostering enduring client relationships.

5.2.1 Pricing Strategies and Negotiation Skills

Setting the right price for your services is essential to reflect your expertise and ensure profitability. Coupled with strong negotiation skills, effective pricing strategies help freelancers secure fair compensation while maintaining client satisfaction.

1. **Determining Your Pricing Structure**
    Freelancers can choose from several pricing models, depending on the nature of their work and client preferences.

    o **Hourly Rates**: Suitable for projects with undefined scopes, where time investment varies.

        ▪ **Calculating Hourly Rates**: Factor in expenses, experience, and regional market standards (e.g., higher rates in the USA or UK compared to global averages).

- **Advantages**: Transparency in billing and adaptability for dynamic projects.

- **Drawbacks**: Limited income potential if tasks are completed more efficiently.

o **Fixed Pricing**: Ideal for well-defined projects with clear deliverables.

- **Project-Based Quotations**: Estimate costs based on complexity, deadlines, and deliverable volume.

- **Advantages**: Predictable income and clarity for both parties.

- **Drawbacks**: Risk of underestimating time or resources required.

o **Value-Based Pricing**: Charging based on the value your work brings to the client.

- **Identifying Value**: Align pricing with potential client outcomes, such as increased revenue or improved brand reputation.

- **Advantages**: Higher earnings potential for skilled freelancers.

- **Drawbacks**: Requires in-depth understanding of client goals and market trends.

2. **Mastering Negotiation Skills**
Effective negotiation ensures fair compensation and strengthens client relationships.

- o **Researching Client Budgets**: Understanding a client's industry and typical budget ranges provides leverage during discussions.

- o **Presenting Value Over Cost**: Emphasise the benefits and outcomes of your work rather than justifying the price.

- o **Handling Pushback Professionally**: Use counteroffers and highlight portfolio success stories to defend your rates.

Subsections for Negotiation Mastery:

- o **Recognising Red Flags**: Beware of clients unwilling to discuss fair terms or offering vague project details.

- o **Offering Tiered Pricing**: Present multiple options (e.g., basic, standard, premium) to cater to different budgets.

- o **Knowing When to Walk Away**: Declining undervalued work demonstrates confidence in your worth.

3. **Adjusting Rates Over Time**
   Regularly revisiting your pricing ensures alignment with market trends and personal growth.

- o **Annual Rate Reviews**: Factor in inflation, new skills, and increased demand for your services.

- o **Communicating Adjustments to Clients**: Notify existing clients of rate changes in advance, highlighting added value.

- o **Benchmarking Against Competitors**: Research industry standards in regions like Europe or the USA for fair pricing.

5.2.2 Finding High-Paying Clients and Retainers

Attracting high-paying clients and securing retainer agreements significantly boosts income stability and growth potential.

---

1. **Targeting High-Value Clients**
   Identifying and approaching clients with substantial budgets maximises earning potential.

   - **Researching Profitable Industries**: Focus on sectors like tech, finance, or healthcare, which often have larger budgets for freelancers.

     - **Regional Insights**: The tech sector thrives in the USA, while sustainability consulting is lucrative in Europe.

   - **Networking in Professional Circles**: Attend industry events or engage in LinkedIn groups to connect with decision-makers.

   - **Leveraging Referrals**: Satisfied clients often refer other high-value opportunities.

2. **Positioning Yourself as a Premium Freelancer**
   Establishing a strong personal brand and showcasing expertise attracts top-tier clients.

   - **Building Authority**: Publish thought leadership content, such as blogs or webinars, to demonstrate industry knowledge.

   - **Showcasing Results**: Highlight measurable outcomes from previous projects, such as increased sales or improved efficiency.

   - **Professional Presentation**: Invest in high-quality branding materials, including a polished website and portfolio.

3. **Securing Retainer Agreements**
   Retainers provide consistent income and foster ongoing client relationships.

- o **Types of Retainers**: Options include monthly deliverables, priority access, or hourly blocks.

- o **Pitching Retainers to Clients**: Emphasise the convenience and reliability of having ongoing access to your services.

- o **Negotiating Terms**: Define clear deliverables, communication protocols, and payment schedules.

Subsections for Retainers:

- o **Transitioning from One-Off Projects**: Use successful collaborations to propose retainer agreements.

- o **Long-Term Benefits**: Predictable income reduces the stress of constant client acquisition.

- o **Monitoring Retainer Performance**: Regularly review and adjust terms to ensure mutual satisfaction.

5.2.3 Building Long-Term Client Relationships

Developing strong client relationships is key to ensuring repeat business, referrals, and a positive reputation.

1. **Providing Exceptional Value**
   Consistently exceeding client expectations fosters trust and loyalty.

   - o **Proactive Communication**: Regular updates and prompt responses demonstrate professionalism.

   - o **Anticipating Client Needs**: Offer solutions or suggestions that address future challenges.

- o **Delivering Quality Work**: Maintain high standards to build confidence in your capabilities.

2. **Establishing Trust and Credibility**
Transparent interactions and reliability strengthen client confidence in your services.

- o **Honouring Commitments**: Meet deadlines and deliverables as promised.

- o **Clarifying Expectations**: Define project scopes and responsibilities upfront to avoid misunderstandings.

- o **Admitting Mistakes**: Take accountability for errors and propose solutions to maintain trust.

3. **Encouraging Client Retention**
Building rapport and maintaining communication encourage clients to continue working with you.

- o **Regular Check-Ins**: Periodically reach out to discuss ongoing or future needs.

- o **Offering Exclusive Benefits**: Provide loyal clients with discounts, priority scheduling, or additional services.

- o **Celebrating Milestones**: Acknowledge anniversaries, project successes, or client achievements to personalise relationships.

Subsections for Retention Strategies:

- o **Upselling Additional Services**: Expand collaborations by offering complementary solutions.

- o **Requesting Feedback**: Use client input to improve services and demonstrate commitment to their success.

- o **Creating Client Loyalty Programmes**: Incentivise repeat business through tailored rewards.

Conclusion

Maximising income as a freelancer involves strategic pricing, attracting high-value clients, and nurturing long-term relationships. By positioning yourself as a premium professional and consistently delivering exceptional value, you can achieve sustainable growth in competitive markets like the USA, UK, Europe, and beyond.

The next section will focus on **Tools and Technologies to Help Provide Remote Freelance Services**, exploring strategies to build a strong personal brand, leverage social media, and expand your client base effectively.

5.3 Tools and Technologies for Remote Work

The shift to remote work has made the adoption of the right tools and technologies crucial for maintaining productivity, collaboration, and organisation. This section explores the essential software and platforms that facilitate effective communication, seamless collaboration, and efficient task management in a remote working environment. By leveraging these technologies, professionals across the USA, UK, Europe, and global markets can thrive in the evolving digital workspace.

5.3.1 Project Management and Communication Tools

Effective project management and clear communication are the cornerstones of remote work. This subsection highlights tools designed to streamline tasks, foster transparency, and enhance team collaboration.

1. **Project Management Platforms**

   These platforms help remote teams plan, organise, and track their work, ensuring projects are completed efficiently.

   o **Trello: Visual Task Management**

     - **How It Works**: Trello uses boards, lists, and cards to create a visual workflow for tasks and projects.

     - **Benefits**: Ideal for smaller teams or freelancers managing individual tasks, with features like deadlines and checklists.

     - **Use Cases**: Trello is widely adopted in the UK and Europe for organising marketing campaigns or editorial calendars.

   o **Asana: Comprehensive Team Coordination**

     - **How It Works**: Asana offers advanced features for project planning, including task dependencies, timelines, and workload views.

     - **Benefits**: Suitable for medium to large teams, ensuring accountability and transparency.

     - **Use Cases**: Common in the USA and global markets for IT projects, software development, and corporate initiatives.

   o **Monday.com: Customisable Workflows**

     - **How It Works**: Monday.com enables teams to create tailored workflows to suit specific industries or project types.

- **Benefits**: Integrates with popular tools like Slack and Google Drive, enhancing overall productivity.

- **Use Cases**: Frequently used in Europe for cross-departmental collaborations in tech startups.

2. **Communication Tools for Remote Teams**
   Real-time and asynchronous communication tools keep teams connected, fostering collaboration regardless of time zones.

   o **Slack: Instant Messaging for Teams**

     - **How It Works**: Slack organises communication into channels based on projects or topics, reducing email clutter.

     - **Benefits**: Supports integrations with project management tools and video conferencing platforms.

     - **Use Cases**: Popular in the USA for tech companies managing distributed teams.

   o **Microsoft Teams: Integrated Collaboration**

     - **How It Works**: Combines chat, video meetings, and file sharing within a single platform.

     - **Benefits**: Seamlessly integrates with Microsoft Office 365, making it ideal for corporate environments.

     - **Use Cases**: Widely adopted in the UK for remote education and government projects.

   o **Zoom: Video Conferencing Leader**

- **How It Works**: Offers high-quality video calls, virtual backgrounds, and breakout rooms for effective meetings.

- **Benefits**: Essential for client presentations, training sessions, and team discussions.

- **Use Cases**: Globally recognised as the go-to platform for webinars and remote conferences.

3. **Tracking and Time Management Tools**
These tools help remote workers monitor productivity and manage time effectively.

    o **Toggl Track**: Tracks work hours for accurate billing and productivity analysis.

    o **RescueTime**: Analyses daily habits to identify productivity bottlenecks.

    o **Clockify**: A free time-tracking tool popular among freelancers managing multiple clients.

5.3.2 Collaboration and Cloud-Based Software

Collaboration tools and cloud-based solutions enable teams to share files, co-create content, and manage resources efficiently, regardless of location.

---

1. **Cloud Storage and File Sharing**
Secure and accessible cloud storage is vital for remote teams handling large volumes of data.

    o **Google Drive**: Offers 15GB of free storage and seamless integration with Google Workspace for document editing and sharing.

- o **Dropbox**: Provides advanced file-sharing options and document recovery features, catering to creative professionals.

- o **OneDrive**: Microsoft's solution integrates with Office 365, making it ideal for businesses using Microsoft tools.

2. **Real-Time Collaboration Tools**
   These platforms allow multiple team members to work on documents or projects simultaneously.

   - o **Google Docs and Sheets**: Real-time editing with robust sharing and commenting features.

   - o **Notion**: Combines note-taking, task management, and database creation in one platform.

   - o **Miro**: A digital whiteboard tool for brainstorming and visual collaboration, widely used in design and strategy sessions.

3. **Security and Compliance in Cloud Solutions**
   Ensuring data security and regulatory compliance is essential for businesses operating across global markets.

   - o **Encryption Standards**: Choose tools with end-to-end encryption to protect sensitive information.

   - o **GDPR Compliance**: Ensure cloud services meet data protection standards, particularly for European clients.

   - o **Backup and Recovery**: Implement systems for data backup to safeguard against loss or corruption.

5.3.3 Staying Productive and Organised Remotely

Maintaining productivity and organisation in a remote work environment requires discipline and the right tools. This subsection explores strategies and software to help remote professionals stay on track.

---

1. **Creating an Organised Workspace**
   A well-structured workspace boosts focus and efficiency.

   - o **Ergonomic Furniture**: Invest in adjustable chairs and desks to prevent strain during long work hours.

   - o **Declutter and Personalise**: Keep your workspace tidy and add personal touches to enhance comfort.

   - o **Technology Setup**: Use dual monitors, noise-cancelling headphones, and reliable internet connections for optimal performance.

2. **Productivity Apps and Techniques**
   Apps and time management techniques help remote workers stay disciplined and meet deadlines.

   - o **Pomodoro Technique**: Use apps like Focus Booster to implement time-blocking strategies.

   - o **Todoist**: A task management app for organising daily to-do lists and setting priorities.

   - o **Habitica**: Gamifies productivity by turning tasks into achievements.

3. **Balancing Work and Life**
   Remote work can blur boundaries between professional and personal time, making balance essential.

   - o **Setting Boundaries**: Establish clear work hours and communicate them to family and clients.

- o **Taking Breaks**: Schedule regular breaks to recharge and avoid burnout.

- o **Mental Health Resources**: Use mindfulness apps like Calm or Headspace to manage stress.

Conclusion

Tools and technologies are integral to successful remote work, enabling seamless collaboration, effective project management, and sustained productivity. By leveraging these solutions, freelancers and remote teams can overcome challenges and achieve their goals in competitive markets like the USA, UK, Europe, and beyond.

The next section will focus on **Freelancing Legal and Financial Considerations**, exploring the essentials of contracts, invoicing, and intellectual property protection to ensure a stable and compliant freelancing career.

5.4 Freelancing Legal and Financial Considerations

Operating as a freelancer involves navigating legal and financial complexities to protect your business and ensure compliance. This section explores the essentials of contracts, payment systems, taxation, and intellectual property protection, providing a comprehensive guide for freelancers in the USA, UK, Europe, and global markets.

5.4.1 Contracts and Client Agreements

Establishing clear, legally binding contracts is fundamental to protecting your rights, outlining expectations, and avoiding disputes. This subsection provides insights into creating and managing effective client agreements.

---

1. **Key Components of a Freelance Contract**
   A well-structured contract safeguards both parties and reduces misunderstandings.

   - **Scope of Work (SOW)**: Clearly define deliverables, deadlines, and responsibilities.

     - **Specificity in Deliverables**: Include detailed descriptions of what the client can expect, such as "10 social media posts" instead of "content creation."

     - **Revisions and Adjustments**: Outline the number of revisions included and the cost of additional changes.

     - **Timeline and Milestones**: Use milestones for larger projects, specifying payment upon completion of each stage.

   - **Payment Terms**: Ensure transparency about fees, payment schedules, and methods.

- **Upfront Deposits**: Requesting a deposit (e.g., 30–50%) protects against non-payment.

- **Late Payment Policies**: Include penalties for overdue invoices to encourage timely payments.

- **Currency and Exchange Rates**: Specify the currency for payment, particularly for international clients.

o **Termination Clauses**: Protect against sudden project cancellations.

- **Client-Initiated Termination**: Define compensation for work completed up to the cancellation point.

- **Freelancer-Initiated Termination**: Include conditions under which you may terminate the agreement, such as breach of contract.

- **Force Majeure**: Cover unforeseeable circumstances, such as natural disasters, that may impede project completion.

2. **Drafting and Reviewing Contracts**
Use templates or consult professionals to ensure your contracts are enforceable and compliant with local laws.

o **Freelance Contract Templates**: Platforms like Bonsai and And.co offer customisable contract templates.

o **Legal Review**: Engage a solicitor or legal consultant for high-value or complex agreements.

o **Adapting for Regional Laws**: Tailor contracts to meet regulations specific to markets like the

UK (GDPR compliance) or the USA (state-specific laws).

3. **Digital Contract Management**
   Leverage technology to simplify contract signing, storage, and retrieval.

   o **Electronic Signatures**: Tools like DocuSign and Adobe Sign streamline the signing process.

   o **Cloud Storage**: Securely store contracts on platforms like Dropbox or Google Drive for easy access.

   o **Contract Management Software**: Use platforms like PandaDoc to automate contract workflows.

5.4.2 Invoicing, Payments, and Taxes

Efficient invoicing and adherence to tax regulations are vital for maintaining a financially stable freelancing business. This subsection covers best practices for managing payments and tax obligations.

---

1. **Creating Professional Invoices**
   Invoicing clients promptly and accurately ensures consistent cash flow.

   o **Essential Invoice Components**: Include your name, contact details, client information, invoice number, and payment terms.

   ▪ **Breakdown of Charges**: Itemise services or deliverables to provide transparency.

   ▪ **Due Dates**: Clearly state the payment deadline to avoid confusion.

- **Tax Information**: Include VAT or sales tax details if applicable.

  o **Using Invoice Generators**: Platforms like Wave and FreshBooks simplify invoice creation and tracking.

  o **Sending Invoices Digitally**: Use email or invoicing software with tracking features to confirm receipt.

  o **Setting Reminders**: Automate reminders for overdue payments to streamline follow-ups.

2. **Choosing Payment Methods**
   Offer multiple payment options to accommodate clients' preferences and expedite transactions.

   o **Bank Transfers**: Widely used in Europe, with SEPA enabling quick transfers within the EU.

   o **Online Payment Platforms**: PayPal and Wise are popular for international payments, offering currency conversion features.

   o **Cryptocurrency Payments**: Accepting crypto provides flexibility for tech-savvy clients but requires volatility management.

3. **Understanding Tax Obligations**
   Freelancers must comply with tax regulations specific to their country of residence and clients' locations.

   o **Income Tax**: Report all earnings to tax authorities, using accounting software like QuickBooks to simplify calculations.

   o **VAT/Sales Tax**: Register for VAT if your turnover exceeds thresholds (e.g., £85,000 in the UK) or if required for EU transactions.

   o **Estimated Tax Payments**: Freelancers in the USA and some EU countries must pay quarterly taxes to avoid penalties.

Subsections for Tax Management:

- o **Tracking Expenses**: Deduct business-related costs, such as equipment, software subscriptions, or home office utilities.

- o **Hiring Accountants**: Engage professionals to navigate complex tax codes and maximise deductions.

- o **Cross-Border Taxes**: Understand double taxation treaties and withholdings for international clients.

5.4.3 Protecting Intellectual Property

Freelancers often create original work that requires intellectual property (IP) protection to prevent unauthorised use or exploitation.

1. **Defining Ownership Rights**
   Specify who owns the rights to deliverables and under what conditions.

   - o **Work-for-Hire Agreements**: Clearly state if the client retains exclusive rights to the work.

   - o **Retaining Usage Rights**: Negotiate terms to use completed work in your portfolio or case studies.

   - o **License Agreements**: Offer non-exclusive licences to clients for limited use of your work.

2. **Copyright Registration**
   Protecting your creations with copyright ensures legal recourse in cases of infringement.

   - o **Registering Copyright**: Apply through regional offices, such as the UK's Intellectual Property Office or the US Copyright Office.

- o **Watermarking Work**: Add watermarks to digital content shared during negotiations to deter unauthorised use.

- o **Tracking Infringement**: Use tools like TinEye or Google Image Search to detect unauthorised usage of your work.

3. **Legal Recourse for IP Infringement**
Understanding your options in cases of copyright violations or disputes is essential.

- o **Sending Cease-and-Desist Letters**: Notify infringers of legal action if they continue to misuse your work.

- o **Mediation and Arbitration**: Resolve disputes through neutral third parties to avoid costly litigation.

- o **Filing Lawsuits**: Pursue legal action in cases of significant financial or reputational harm.

Conclusion

Managing legal and financial considerations is crucial for a sustainable freelancing business. By drafting clear contracts, streamlining payments, ensuring tax compliance, and protecting intellectual property, freelancers can safeguard their work and income across markets in the USA, UK, Europe, and beyond.

The next chapter, **Investment Opportunities in the Digital World**, will explore strategies for leveraging digital real estate, buying and selling online assets, and generating passive income through digital investments.

Chapter 6: Investment Opportunities in the Digital World

The digital revolution has reshaped investment landscapes, offering opportunities that were unimaginable just a few decades ago. From owning virtual properties in the metaverse to building portfolios of digital assets, the digital economy has opened doors for individuals and businesses to create wealth in innovative ways. This chapter explores key investment strategies in the digital realm, focusing on areas such as digital real estate, crowdfunding, and passive income models.

As traditional investments continue to evolve, the allure of digital opportunities lies in their accessibility, scalability, and potential for high returns. Whether you are based in the USA, the UK, Europe, or elsewhere, the strategies and insights outlined in this chapter will help you navigate the fast-paced world of digital investments and capitalise on its potential.

The Rise of Digital Investments

The shift from physical to digital assets reflects the growing influence of technology on global markets. Digital investments often provide lower entry barriers, greater flexibility, and a global reach.

1. **Accessibility and Inclusion**
   The digital economy has democratised investing, enabling individuals from diverse backgrounds to participate.

   o **Global Access**: Platforms like Flippa, Empire Flippers, and OpenSea cater to investors from around the world.

   o **Low Entry Barriers**: Unlike traditional real estate, digital properties can often be acquired at lower costs.

- o **Skill-Based Opportunities**: Knowledge of SEO, web design, or content creation enhances the profitability of digital investments.

2. **Technological Advancements**
Innovation has driven the development of tools and platforms that facilitate digital investments.

- o **Blockchain Technology**: Ensures transparency and security in transactions, especially for virtual real estate and NFTs.

- o **Automation Tools**: Platforms like Shopify and WordPress simplify management for e-commerce and content sites.

- o **Crowdfunding Ecosystems**: Websites like Kickstarter and Patreon enable collaborative investment ventures.

3. **Global Trends in Digital Investing**
The popularity of digital investments varies across regions, reflecting local market conditions and technological adoption.

- o **USA**: A hub for innovation, with significant activity in NFTs, crowdfunding, and e-commerce platforms.

- o **UK**: Focused on digital real estate and content monetisation, supported by robust online infrastructure.

- o **Europe**: Sustainability and green tech investments are growing, integrating digital platforms with environmental goals.

Opportunities and Challenges

While digital investments offer significant potential, they also come with unique challenges that require careful navigation.

1. **Opportunities**

   o **Scalability**: Digital investments often require minimal incremental costs to scale.

   o **Diverse Income Streams**: Combine affiliate marketing, ad revenue, and subscription models to maximise returns.

   o **Global Reach**: Reach customers or audiences worldwide without the limitations of physical borders.

2. **Challenges**

   o **Volatility**: Digital asset markets, especially in areas like NFTs or cryptocurrencies, can fluctuate significantly.

   o **Regulatory Uncertainty**: Varying laws around digital asset ownership and taxation require vigilance.

   o **Competition**: The digital investment space is increasingly saturated, necessitating strategic differentiation.

Why Now is the Time to Invest Digitally

The rapid digital transformation accelerated by the pandemic has made the digital economy an integral part of global commerce. With new opportunities emerging daily, now is an opportune moment to engage with digital investments.

1. **Accelerated Growth**
   The global adoption of digital platforms has created fertile ground for investments.

   o **E-Commerce Expansion**: Platforms like Amazon and Etsy have seen exponential growth, creating demand for supporting services.

- o **Metaverse Development**: Companies like Meta and Decentraland are investing heavily in virtual spaces.

2. **Changing Consumer Behaviours**
Increasing reliance on digital platforms for shopping, entertainment, and education creates new markets for investors.

- o **Digital Content Consumption**: Streaming, gaming, and online learning have become major revenue-generating sectors.

- o **Sustainability Trends**: Consumers value businesses with a commitment to ethical and sustainable practices, opening opportunities for green tech investments.

3. **Building a Future-Proof Portfolio**
Diversifying into digital assets ensures adaptability to future market changes.

- o **Resilience in Economic Downturns**: Digital assets often provide alternative revenue streams during economic uncertainty.

- o **Innovation-Led Growth**: Investing in cutting-edge technologies keeps portfolios aligned with emerging trends.

Conclusion

As the digital economy continues to expand, so do the opportunities for investment. Whether you're looking to generate passive income, diversify your portfolio, or venture into innovative spaces like the metaverse, understanding the nuances of digital investments is essential. The subsequent sections of this chapter will explore specific opportunities, such as digital real estate, website flipping, crowdfunding, and passive income strategies, offering actionable insights for success in the digital world.

Let's break this down in more detail.

6.1 Investing in Digital Real Estate

Digital real estate has emerged as a lucrative asset class in the modern economy, encompassing domain names, websites, and virtual properties within the metaverse. Unlike physical real estate, digital assets offer global reach, lower entry barriers, and unique opportunities for creative monetisation. This section delves into the intricacies of investing in digital real estate, including strategies for domain flipping, navigating the metaverse, and leveraging digital properties for passive income.

6.1.1 Domain Flipping and Website Investments

Domain names and websites are the building blocks of the internet. Investing in these assets can yield substantial returns when managed strategically.

1. **Understanding Domain Flipping**
   Domain flipping involves buying domain names at a low cost and selling them for profit. This practice requires foresight, research, and marketing skills.

   o **Identifying Valuable Domains**: Domains with short, memorable names or high search relevance often fetch premium prices.

     ▪ **Keyword-Rich Domains**: Examples include "BestLondonHotels.com" or "DigitalMarketingTips.com," which rank well in search engines.

     ▪ **Brandable Names**: Unique, catchy names that businesses can adopt, such as "BrandHive.com."

- **Niche Domains**: Target specific industries or trends, such as "SustainableTech.net" for eco-focused companies.

  o **Buying Domains**: Platforms like GoDaddy, Namecheap, and Sedo allow investors to search for and purchase domains.

  - **Expired Domains**: Look for domains with existing backlinks or search engine authority.

  - **Auctions**: Participate in domain auctions to acquire high-value assets at competitive prices.

  o **Selling Domains**: Once acquired, domains can be sold through marketplaces or directly to interested buyers.

  - **Marketplaces**: Platforms like Flippa and Afternic connect sellers with buyers worldwide.

  - **Direct Sales**: Approach businesses that might benefit from a specific domain name.

  - **Pricing Strategies**: Set prices based on metrics like traffic, SEO value, and industry relevance.

2. **Website Investments**
   Websites with established traffic and revenue streams offer higher earning potential than standalone domains.

   o **Buying Websites**: Evaluate websites on platforms like Empire Flippers, FE International, or Motion Invest.

- **Metrics to Assess**: Traffic sources, revenue streams (e.g., ads, affiliate links), and SEO performance.
- **Industry Trends**: Focus on growing niches, such as e-learning or health and wellness.
- **Valuation Models**: Websites are often priced at 20–40 times their monthly earnings.

o **Improving Website Value**: Enhancing website performance increases profitability and resale value.

- **Content Optimisation**: Publish high-quality, engaging articles to attract organic traffic.
- **User Experience**: Improve website design, speed, and navigation for better engagement.
- **Diversifying Income Streams**: Introduce additional revenue methods, such as subscriptions or sponsored posts.

o **Selling Websites**: When the value peaks, websites can be sold for a profit.

- **Exit Strategies**: Plan sales during market highs or after achieving growth milestones.
- **Due Diligence**: Prepare financial records and analytics data to assure buyers of the site's profitability.

3. **Risks and Rewards**
Investing in domains and websites involves balancing potential gains against inherent risks.

- o **Rewards**:

  - ▪ **High Profit Margins**: Successful domain flips or websites can yield significant returns.

  - ▪ **Recurring Revenue**: Websites with ad or affiliate income provide consistent earnings.

- o **Risks**:

  - ▪ **Market Volatility**: Demand for specific domains or niches may fluctuate.

  - ▪ **Competition**: Established investors often dominate premium markets.

6.1.2 Virtual Real Estate in the Metaverse

Virtual real estate refers to properties within online worlds, where users can buy, sell, and develop land for personal or commercial purposes. The metaverse offers unprecedented opportunities for digital entrepreneurs and investors.

1. **The Concept of Virtual Real Estate**
   Virtual properties exist within decentralised platforms like Decentraland, The Sandbox, or Somnium Space.

   - o **Digital Ownership**: Land parcels are represented by NFTs (non-fungible tokens) stored on the blockchain.

   - o **Decentralised Economies**: Users can monetise properties through events, advertising, or virtual storefronts.

   - o **Scarcity Models**: Platforms limit the number of available plots, driving up demand.

2. **How to Buy Virtual Land**
Purchasing virtual real estate requires navigating specific platforms and marketplaces.

- **Selecting a Platform**: Research platforms based on user activity, community engagement, and development tools.

- **Using Cryptocurrency**: Transactions are typically conducted in cryptocurrencies like Ethereum (ETH) or MANA (Decentraland's currency).

- **Evaluating Land Value**: Factors include proximity to landmarks, traffic potential, and development rights.

3. **Developing Virtual Properties**
Similar to physical real estate, virtual properties can be enhanced to increase their value.

- **Building Infrastructure**: Create interactive spaces like art galleries, event venues, or gaming areas.

- **Hosting Events**: Charge entry fees for virtual concerts, conferences, or exhibitions.

- **Advertising Space**: Lease ad spots to businesses seeking exposure to metaverse audiences.

4. **Challenges in Virtual Real Estate**
While lucrative, investing in virtual real estate carries unique challenges.

- **Regulatory Uncertainty**: Governments are still defining legal frameworks for virtual assets.

- **Platform Dependence**: Value is tied to the success and longevity of the hosting platform.

- **Market Speculation**: Prices can fluctuate based on hype and investor sentiment.

6.1.3 Monetising Digital Properties

Owning digital properties opens up diverse avenues for generating revenue. This subsection explores strategies to maximise returns.

1. **Advertising Revenue**
   Digital properties with high traffic or visibility can generate income through ads.

   o **Direct Ad Sales**: Partner with brands seeking exposure in your niche.

   o **Ad Networks**: Platforms like Google AdSense or Media.net automate ad placement for consistent earnings.

   o **Sponsored Content**: Collaborate with businesses to create tailored content campaigns.

2. **Subscription Models**
   Offering premium content or exclusive access incentivises users to pay recurring fees.

   o **Membership Websites**: Restrict access to high-value resources, tutorials, or forums.

   o **Patreon Integration**: Creators can monetise content by engaging directly with subscribers.

   o **Freemium Models**: Provide basic services for free while charging for advanced features.

3. **E-Commerce Integration**
   Digital properties can host online stores, expanding revenue streams.

   o **Dropshipping**: Sell products without holding inventory, using platforms like Shopify.

- o **Digital Products**: Offer e-books, courses, or software directly through the property.

- o **Affiliate Marketing**: Earn commissions by promoting third-party products or services.

4. **Licensing Intellectual Property**
Properties with unique designs or branding can be licensed to other users or companies.

- o **Licensing Agreements**: Charge fees for the use of content, designs, or functionality.

- o **Creative Commons**: Share assets under specific usage terms to generate exposure and revenue.

Conclusion

Investing in digital real estate offers unparalleled opportunities for generating income and building wealth. From flipping domains and managing websites to owning virtual properties in the metaverse, the possibilities are vast and ever-evolving. With careful research, strategic planning, and a proactive approach to monetisation, individuals in the USA, UK, Europe, and global markets can thrive in this dynamic sector.

The next section will focus on **Buying and Selling Websites and Apps**, providing insights into platforms, valuation metrics, and risk management for profitable investments in digital assets.

6.2 Buying and Selling Websites and Apps

The market for websites and apps has grown into a thriving sector within the digital economy, offering entrepreneurs and investors opportunities to acquire profitable assets or sell established projects. This section explores platforms for buying and selling, valuation metrics for assessing digital assets, and due diligence strategies to mitigate risks and ensure successful transactions.

6.2.1 Platforms for Buying/Selling Websites and Apps

The rise of specialised platforms has simplified the process of buying and selling websites and apps. These marketplaces connect buyers and sellers, provide valuation tools, and facilitate secure transactions.

1. **Flippa: A Leading Marketplace**
   Flippa is one of the most popular platforms for trading websites, apps, and domains.

   o **Overview of Flippa**

- **Global Reach**: Flippa connects buyers and sellers from the USA, UK, Europe, and beyond.

- **Diverse Listings**: Offers everything from content sites and e-commerce stores to SaaS products.

- **User-Friendly Tools**: Provides valuation tools and analytics to support informed decisions.

- **Key Features**

  - **Auction System**: Buyers bid on listings, driving competitive pricing for sellers.

  - **Negotiation Options**: Direct negotiation between parties ensures flexible terms.

  - **Verification Services**: Flippa offers optional due diligence reports for added security.

- **How to Succeed on Flippa**

  - **For Buyers**: Set a clear budget and use filters to target profitable niches.

  - **For Sellers**: Present detailed financials and highlight unique selling points (USPs).

2. **Empire Flippers: A Premium Option**
   Empire Flippers caters to high-value transactions, specialising in established websites and e-commerce businesses.

   - **Overview of Empire Flippers**

     - **High-Quality Listings**: Focuses on websites and apps with proven revenue streams.

- **Curated Marketplace**: All listings undergo a vetting process to ensure quality.

- **Global Transactions**: Popular among buyers in Europe and the USA seeking reliable investments.

  o **Key Features**

    - **Valuation Tools**: Empire Flippers provides detailed financial breakdowns for each listing.

    - **Buyer Vetting**: Ensures serious inquiries, reducing time-wasting negotiations.

    - **Post-Sale Support**: Offers migration assistance for seamless ownership transitions.

  o **Best Practices**

    - **For Buyers**: Leverage Empire Flippers' vetting to focus on high-quality assets.

    - **For Sellers**: Prepare comprehensive documentation to pass the vetting process.

3. **Alternative Platforms**
   Beyond Flippa and Empire Flippers, other platforms cater to niche markets or specific asset types.

   o **MicroAcquire**: Targets SaaS startups and tech-driven businesses.

   o **FE International**: Specialises in mergers and acquisitions, ideal for high-value deals.

   o **Motion Invest**: Aims at smaller transactions, appealing to first-time buyers.

Subsections for Alternative Platforms:

- o **Platform Comparisons**: Evaluate costs, features, and niches.

- o **Regional Preferences**: Identify platforms popular in specific markets, such as Europe or Asia.

- o **Emerging Marketplaces**: Keep an eye on new platforms catering to innovative digital assets.

6.2.2 Valuation Metrics for Digital Assets

Proper valuation is critical for determining the worth of a website or app. This subsection outlines key metrics and methodologies to ensure fair pricing.

1. **Revenue and Profitability Metrics**
   Financial performance is a primary determinant of a digital asset's value.

   - o **Monthly Recurring Revenue (MRR)**: Websites or apps with subscription models are often valued based on MRR.

   - o **Net Profit**: Calculate profit by deducting operational expenses from total revenue.

   - o **Earnings Multiples**: Assets are typically priced at 20–50 times their monthly net profit.

2. **Traffic and User Engagement**
   The quantity and quality of traffic directly impact a website or app's earning potential.

   - o **Traffic Sources**: Organic traffic from search engines is more valuable than paid traffic.

   - o **Bounce Rate**: Low bounce rates indicate user engagement and content relevance.

- o **Retention Metrics**: For apps, high retention rates and daily active users (DAU) signal strong user loyalty.

3. **Niche and Market Trends**
   Certain niches and trends command higher valuations due to demand and growth potential.

   - o **High-Demand Niches**: Examples include fitness apps, e-learning platforms, and finance blogs.

   - o **Emerging Trends**: Keep an eye on sectors like blockchain-based apps or eco-conscious e-commerce sites.

   - o **Geographical Trends**: Websites catering to European sustainability initiatives or US tech hubs may attract premium buyers.

6.2.3 Due Diligence and Risk Assessment

Conducting thorough due diligence reduces the risk of purchasing undervalued or problematic assets. This subsection provides a checklist for evaluating websites and apps.

---

1. **Analysing Financial Records**
   Verify the accuracy of revenue and expense data to assess profitability.

   - o **Profit and Loss Statements**: Review detailed reports spanning at least 12 months.

   - o **Third-Party Integrations**: Cross-check analytics data from tools like Google Analytics or Stripe.

   - o **Recurring Expenses**: Identify hidden costs, such as hosting fees or ad spend.

2. **Evaluating Traffic and SEO Metrics**
   Ensure the website or app generates sustainable and legitimate traffic.

   o **Traffic Consistency**: Look for stable or growing trends over time.

   o **SEO Health**: Analyse backlink profiles, domain authority, and keyword rankings.

   o **Red Flags**: Watch for sudden traffic spikes from suspicious sources.

3. **Assessing Operational and Technical Risks**
   Understand the technical infrastructure and potential challenges.

   o **Code Review**: Ensure app code is well-documented and free of vulnerabilities.

   o **Platform Dependencies**: Identify reliance on third-party services that could disrupt operations.

   o **Legal Compliance**: Verify adherence to GDPR (Europe), CCPA (USA), or other regional regulations.

4. **Negotiating and Structuring Deals**
   Secure favourable terms to protect your investment.

   o **Escrow Services**: Use platforms like Escrow.com to hold funds until transaction completion.

   o **Contingency Clauses**: Include terms for addressing undisclosed issues post-sale.

   o **Payment Plans**: Negotiate instalments for high-value purchases to reduce upfront risk.

Conclusion

Buying and selling websites and apps is a dynamic field that rewards diligent research, strategic valuation, and effective negotiation. By leveraging trusted platforms, applying robust valuation techniques, and conducting thorough due diligence, investors can minimise risks and maximise returns. This approach ensures success in markets across the USA, UK, Europe, and globally.

The next section will explore **Crowdfunding and Peer-to-Peer Lending**, offering insights into collaborative investment opportunities and assessing their potential within the digital economy.

6.3 Crowdfunding and Peer-to-Peer Lending

Crowdfunding and peer-to-peer (P2P) lending have revolutionised the way individuals and businesses access capital. These methods leverage digital platforms to connect fundraisers with backers, offering diverse opportunities for investment and collaboration. This section explores the primary types of crowdfunding, evaluates the risks and rewards of P2P lending, and highlights popular platforms in global markets.

6.3.1 Types of Crowdfunding: Rewards, Equity, and Debt-Based

Crowdfunding is a versatile model that allows individuals and organisations to raise funds for various projects. Understanding the different types of crowdfunding is key to identifying suitable opportunities for investment or fundraising.

1. **Rewards-Based Crowdfunding**
   Rewards-based crowdfunding offers contributors non-financial incentives in exchange for their support.

   o **How it Works:**

- Backers contribute funds to a project and receive rewards such as products, services, or experiences in return.

- Popular for creative projects, tech startups, and small-scale ventures.

- **Advantages**:

  - **Low Risk for Fundraisers**: No repayment or equity exchange is required.

  - **Engaged Communities**: Backers often act as brand ambassadors, promoting projects to wider audiences.

- **Challenges**:

  - **Delivery Delays**: Fulfilling rewards can be time-consuming and costly.

  - **Uncertain Outcomes**: Investors face risks if projects fail to deliver on promises.

Subsections for Rewards-Based Crowdfunding:

- **Case Studies**: Successful campaigns like Pebble Watch and Exploding Kittens.

- **Best Practices**: Effective storytelling, detailed timelines, and attractive rewards.

- **Popular Platforms**: Kickstarter (USA, UK) and Indiegogo (global).

2. **Equity Crowdfunding**
   Equity crowdfunding allows backers to invest in exchange for ownership stakes in a company.

   - **How it Works**:

     - Investors receive shares proportional to their contributions.

- Typically used by startups or early-stage businesses.

  o **Advantages**:

    - **Potential for High Returns**: Equity can appreciate significantly if the business succeeds.

    - **Active Participation**: Investors may provide strategic advice or networking opportunities.

  o **Challenges**:

    - **High Risk**: Startups often face significant failure rates.

    - **Dilution of Shares**: Subsequent funding rounds can reduce ownership percentages.

Subsections for Equity Crowdfunding:

  o **Legal Frameworks**: Regulations in the USA (SEC), UK (FCA), and Europe (EU crowdfunding regulations).

  o **Success Stories**: BrewDog (UK) and Oculus Rift (USA).

  o **Platform Examples**: Seedrs (UK), Crowdcube (UK), and StartEngine (USA).

3. **Debt-Based Crowdfunding**
   Also known as peer-to-business (P2B) lending, debt-based crowdfunding provides loans to businesses or individuals.

   o **How it Works**:

     - Fundraisers borrow money from backers and repay it with interest.

- Commonly used for small businesses, real estate, or personal loans.

  o **Advantages**:

    - **Predictable Returns**: Investors receive regular interest payments.

    - **Lower Risk than Equity**: Loans are often secured by collateral.

  o **Challenges**:

    - **Default Risks**: Borrowers may fail to repay.

    - **Regulatory Complexity**: Compliance with lending laws varies by region.

Subsections for Debt-Based Crowdfunding:

  o **Risk Mitigation**: Strategies for assessing borrower creditworthiness.

  o **Emerging Trends**: Green loans and microfinancing initiatives.

  o **Platforms to Watch**: Funding Circle (UK, USA) and LendingClub (USA).

6.3.2 Risks and Returns of P2P Lending

P2P lending connects borrowers directly with investors, bypassing traditional banks. While it offers attractive returns, it also entails unique risks.

1. **Understanding P2P Lending**

   o **How it Works**:

      - Investors lend money to individuals or businesses via online platforms.

      - Loans are repaid with interest over a fixed term.

   o **Why It's Popular**:

      - Offers higher returns than savings accounts or bonds.

      - Democratizes access to credit for underserved demographics.

2. **Assessing Risks in P2P Lending**

   o **Default Risks**: Borrowers may fail to repay due to financial difficulties.

   o **Platform Reliability**: Platform bankruptcy or fraud can jeopardise investments.

   o **Regulatory Risks**: Compliance varies by country, affecting investor protections.

Subsections for Risk Assessment:

   o **Diversification Strategies**: Spread investments across multiple loans and borrowers.

   o **Evaluating Borrower Profiles**: Analyse credit scores, income stability, and loan purposes.

   o **Platform Due Diligence**: Choose reputable platforms with transparent operations.

3. **Potential Returns on P2P Lending**

- o **Interest Rates**: Typically range from 4% to 15%, depending on borrower risk profiles.

- o **Passive Income Opportunities**: Regular repayments can supplement income streams.

- o **Tax Implications**: Interest income may be taxable; check regulations in your region.

6.3.3 Crowdfunding Platforms and Opportunities

The digital landscape is teeming with crowdfunding platforms tailored to various needs and industries. This subsection highlights key platforms and emerging trends.

1. **Top Platforms by Region**

- o **USA**: Kickstarter, Indiegogo, LendingClub.

- o **UK**: Seedrs, Crowdcube, Funding Circle.

- o **Europe**: Ulule (France), Zopa (UK), and Companisto (Germany).

Subsections for Platform Insights:

- o **Specialisation**: Focus areas such as creative projects, tech startups, or real estate.

- o **User Demographics**: Platforms catering to specific age groups or professional backgrounds.

- o **Fee Structures**: Platform commissions and additional charges.

2. **Emerging Trends in Crowdfunding**

   o **Green Crowdfunding**: Backing renewable energy and sustainability projects.

   o **Blockchain Integration**: Leveraging smart contracts for transparent funding.

   o **Hyper-Local Campaigns**: Supporting community-driven initiatives.

3. **Success Factors for Fundraisers and Investors**

   o **For Fundraisers**: Craft compelling pitches, use professional visuals, and engage backers regularly.

   o **For Investors**: Focus on projects aligned with personal values or market trends.

   o **Case Studies**: Highlight successful campaigns that exceeded funding goals.

Conclusion

Crowdfunding and P2P lending represent powerful tools for raising capital and earning returns in the digital economy. By understanding the nuances of different crowdfunding types, evaluating P2P lending risks, and leveraging top platforms, individuals and businesses can tap into these innovative financing methods to achieve their goals.

The next section, **Passive Income through Digital Investments**, will delve into strategies for generating consistent revenue from digital assets such as affiliate websites, subscription models, and digital products.

6.4 Passive Income through Digital Investments

Passive income strategies in the digital economy have become increasingly appealing as they offer scalable and sustainable ways to generate revenue. From affiliate websites to subscription models and digital products, these investments allow individuals and businesses to create income streams that require minimal ongoing effort after initial setup. This section explores three major avenues for generating passive income through digital investments, providing insights into their opportunities, challenges, and global applicability.

6.4.1 Affiliate Websites and Content Sites

Affiliate marketing has revolutionised the way individuals earn online by leveraging partnerships with brands to promote products and earn commissions. Content-rich websites remain one of the most effective platforms for affiliate marketing, driving organic traffic and maximising conversions.

1. **Understanding Affiliate Marketing**
   Affiliate marketing connects content creators with brands seeking to expand their reach.
   - **How It Works**:
     - Website owners join affiliate programmes, receive unique links, and earn a percentage of sales generated through those links.
     - Examples include promoting products on Amazon Associates or niche-specific platforms.

- o **Advantages**:
  - **Scalability**: With consistent traffic, income grows proportionally without additional labour.
  - **Diverse Niches**: Opportunities exist in almost every sector, from fashion and fitness to technology and travel.
- o **Challenges**:
  - **Traffic Dependency**: Success hinges on attracting and retaining a significant audience.
  - **Platform Competition**: High competition in popular niches requires strategic differentiation.

2. **Building Profitable Affiliate Websites**
The foundation of a successful affiliate site lies in its ability to attract, engage, and convert users.

- o **Choosing a Niche**: Focus on industries with high demand and moderate competition.
  - Examples: Personal finance in the USA, sustainable living in Europe, and fitness trends globally.
- o **Creating Quality Content**: Publish in-depth articles, reviews, and guides that address audience pain points.
- o **SEO Optimisation**: Use tools like Ahrefs and SEMrush to target relevant keywords and improve search rankings.

Subsections for Building Websites:

- o **Monetising with Multiple Affiliates**: Work with a mix of affiliate programmes to diversify income sources.

- o **Enhancing User Experience**: Simplify navigation, improve page loading speeds, and ensure mobile compatibility.

- o **Leveraging Analytics**: Track performance using tools like Google Analytics to refine strategies.

3. **Case Studies of Successful Affiliate Sites**
Learning from established websites provides valuable insights.

- o **Wirecutter (USA)**: A consumer product review site earning millions annually through affiliate links.

- o **MoneySavingExpert (UK)**: Focused on personal finance advice, with substantial affiliate earnings.

- o **GreenGeeks (Global)**: A niche hosting affiliate site catering to eco-conscious users.

6.4.2 Subscription Models and Membership Sites

Recurring revenue models have become a cornerstone of digital investments, offering predictable income streams while fostering long-term customer relationships.

---

1. **The Appeal of Subscription Models**

   Subscription-based services cater to customers seeking consistent access to valuable content or services.

   - **How It Works**:
     - Users pay a regular fee (monthly or annually) for access to exclusive content, tools, or communities.
     - Common examples include streaming services like Netflix and specialised platforms like Skillshare.

   - **Advantages**:
     - **Predictable Income**: Regular payments ensure steady cash flow.
     - **Customer Retention**: Subscribers often remain loyal due to convenience and value.

   - **Challenges**:
     - **Churn Rates**: Retaining customers requires consistent value delivery.
     - **Initial Setup Costs**: Developing quality content or services demands upfront investment.

2. **Creating a Membership Site**

   Membership sites cater to niche audiences by offering exclusive benefits.

   - **Content Types**: Webinars, courses, downloadable resources, and forums are popular membership offerings.
   - **Technology Platforms**: Tools like MemberPress (WordPress) and Teachable streamline the creation process.

- o **Pricing Strategies**: Tiered memberships (e.g., basic, premium) cater to different budgets.

Subsections for Membership Sites:

- o **Engaging Members**: Foster a sense of community through interactive features like live Q&A sessions.

- o **Scaling Memberships**: Use referral programmes or ads to grow your subscriber base.

- o **Evaluating Performance**: Track retention rates and member feedback to improve offerings.

3. **Examples of Successful Subscription Models**
   These platforms demonstrate the power of recurring revenue strategies.

- o **Patreon (Global)**: A platform enabling creators to monetise their work through subscriber support.

- o **Headspace (UK)**: Offers mindfulness and meditation resources via a subscription model.

- o **Strava (USA)**: Provides advanced fitness tracking tools for premium members.

6.4.3 Digital Products and E-books

Creating and selling digital products is a low-cost, high-margin strategy for generating passive income. E-books, in particular, have gained popularity due to their ease of creation and distribution.

1. **The Benefits of Selling Digital Products**
   Digital products are scalable, cost-effective, and accessible to creators in any industry.

- **Types of Digital Products**:

    - E-books: Guides or manuals on specific topics, such as personal finance or cooking.

    - Templates: Business plans, resume formats, or social media content calendars.

    - Software: Apps, plugins, or tools tailored to niche audiences.

- **Advantages**:

    - **Minimal Overheads**: No production or inventory costs.

    - **Global Reach**: Platforms like Amazon Kindle and Gumroad enable worldwide sales.

- **Challenges**:

    - **Saturated Markets**: Standing out requires unique value propositions.

    - **Piracy Risks**: Protecting intellectual property can be difficult.

2. **Developing and Marketing E-books**
E-books remain a versatile and lucrative digital product for entrepreneurs and content creators.

    - **Choosing Topics**: Research audience needs and trending subjects.

    - **Designing for Impact**: Use tools like Canva or Adobe InDesign to create visually appealing layouts.

    - **Optimising Distribution**: Leverage platforms like Kindle Direct Publishing (KDP) for Amazon or sell directly via your website.

Subsections for E-book Success:

- o **Pricing Strategies**: Offer competitive pricing, with options for bundled sales.

- o **Promotional Campaigns**: Use email marketing, social media ads, and influencer partnerships.

- o **Customer Engagement**: Gather reviews and testimonials to build credibility.

3. **Expanding Digital Product Portfolios**
   Scaling your offerings enhances revenue potential.

- o **Cross-Promotion**: Bundle e-books with related products, such as online courses.

- o **Collaborations**: Partner with influencers or businesses to co-create products.

- o **Frequent Updates**: Keep content relevant and valuable to maintain sales momentum.

Conclusion

Passive income through digital investments offers unparalleled flexibility and scalability, making it an attractive option for individuals and businesses worldwide. By mastering affiliate marketing, building subscription models, and creating digital products, investors can establish sustainable income streams with global appeal.

The next chapter will explore **The Future of Digital Opportunities**, examining emerging trends, technologies, and strategies for navigating the evolving digital economy.

Chapter 7: The Future of Digital Opportunities

The digital economy continues to evolve at an unprecedented pace, reshaping industries, employment, and everyday life across the globe. Emerging technologies such as artificial intelligence (AI), blockchain, and the Internet of Things (IoT) are not just influencing how businesses operate but are also creating entirely new avenues for innovation and growth. As the lines between physical and virtual worlds blur, understanding these trends and their implications is essential for individuals and businesses seeking to stay ahead of the curve.

This chapter explores the future of digital opportunities, focusing on the transformative technologies, economic shifts, and societal changes that will shape the decades to come. Whether you are navigating the dynamic markets of the USA, the tech hubs of the UK, the innovative ecosystems of Europe, or emerging digital economies globally, this chapter will provide a framework for recognising and leveraging future trends in the digital economy.

The Digital Economy's Rapid Transformation

The rise of digital technology has been one of the most significant economic drivers of the 21st century. What began as the digitisation of traditional industries has expanded into a full-fledged digital revolution.

1. **The Role of Emerging Technologies**
   Breakthroughs in technology are redefining business models, consumer behaviours, and workplace dynamics.

   o **AI and Machine Learning**: These technologies automate processes, personalise user experiences, and enable predictive analytics.

   o **Blockchain**: Beyond cryptocurrency, blockchain ensures secure transactions and decentralised systems in finance, supply chains, and more.

- **IoT**: Connecting everyday objects to the internet fosters smart cities, homes, and devices, transforming how we interact with technology.

2. **Regional Impacts of Digital Transformation**
The scope and speed of digital adoption vary across regions, reflecting unique challenges and opportunities.

   - **USA**: A leader in tech innovation, focusing on AI, cloud computing, and the gig economy.

   - **UK**: Strong in fintech, digital health, and creative industries, supported by robust infrastructure and policy frameworks.

   - **Europe**: Emphasising sustainability and green technologies alongside digital growth.

   - **Global Markets**: Emerging economies like India, Brazil, and Nigeria are leveraging digital solutions to leapfrog traditional development hurdles.

3. **Shifting Workforce Dynamics**
The future of work will increasingly rely on digital platforms, remote collaborations, and reskilling initiatives.

   - **Remote Work Continuation**: The pandemic has normalised flexible working, supported by tools like Zoom and Slack.

   - **Digital Gig Economy**: Freelance platforms such as Upwork and Fiverr enable global talent to connect with opportunities.

   - **Reskilling Needs**: As automation replaces routine jobs, professionals must focus on acquiring in-demand skills like data analysis, coding, and digital marketing.

Opportunities in the Evolving Digital Landscape

The digital economy's growth brings both challenges and opportunities. Recognising trends early and adapting to them can create pathways for success.

1. **Expanding Market Horizons**
   Global digitalisation opens up new markets for businesses and individuals.

   o **Cross-Border E-Commerce**: Platforms like Amazon and Alibaba allow businesses to reach international customers.

   o **Virtual Marketplaces**: The rise of the metaverse introduces immersive shopping and networking experiences.

   o **Digital Content Demand**: Streaming services, online education, and gaming continue to grow, creating opportunities for content creators and developers.

2. **Sustainable Innovation**
   As environmental concerns grow, digital solutions play a pivotal role in addressing global challenges.

   o **Green Technologies**: Renewable energy and eco-friendly innovations are increasingly supported by AI and IoT.

   o **Circular Economy Models**: Blockchain ensures transparency and efficiency in supply chain management for sustainable goods.

   o **Global Collaboration**: Platforms like OpenIDEO facilitate cooperative solutions to pressing environmental issues.

3. **Technological Democratisation**
   Reduced costs and increased accessibility to technology empower individuals and small businesses.

- o **Open-Source Platforms**: Enable innovation without heavy investment in proprietary technologies.

- o **Freemium Models**: Allow users to access basic features at no cost while offering premium upgrades.

- o **Global Skill Sharing**: Platforms like Coursera and Khan Academy provide free or affordable training to millions.

Conclusion

The future of digital opportunities lies in embracing innovation, adapting to change, and recognising the global potential of emerging technologies. From AI-driven automation to the sustainable applications of blockchain, the digital economy is ripe with possibilities for those prepared to navigate its complexities. This chapter will delve deeper into the transformative trends shaping the digital economy and provide actionable insights to help readers position themselves for long-term success.

Next, we will explore **Emerging Technologies and Trends**, focusing on how advancements in artificial intelligence, virtual reality, and sustainability are driving the next phase of the digital revolution.

7.1 Emerging Technologies and Trends

The rapid evolution of technology continues to redefine industries and reshape societies worldwide. Emerging technologies such as artificial intelligence (AI), virtual reality (VR), augmented reality (AR), and the Internet of Things (IoT) are not only transforming digital experiences but also creating new opportunities and challenges. This section examines these advancements, their growing role in digital business, and the shift towards sustainable and green economic trends.

7.1.1 Artificial Intelligence, VR/AR, and IoT

These cutting-edge technologies are driving innovation across various sectors, from healthcare and education to entertainment and commerce. Understanding their potential is crucial for navigating the future digital landscape.

1. **Artificial Intelligence (AI)**
   AI is revolutionising how businesses operate and how individuals interact with technology.

   o **Applications of AI**:

      ▪ **Automation**: AI-powered systems streamline repetitive tasks, such as customer support through chatbots.

      ▪ **Data Analytics**: Predictive analytics enables businesses to forecast trends and personalise user experiences.

      ▪ **Creative AI**: Tools like DALL-E and ChatGPT empower content creators with automated assistance.

- **Global Impact**:
  - **USA**: AI adoption leads in sectors like autonomous vehicles and healthcare diagnostics.
  - **UK**: Focuses on AI ethics and regulation, particularly in finance and government applications.
  - **Europe**: Advances in AI for environmental monitoring and manufacturing.

- **Challenges**:
  - **Data Privacy**: Balancing innovation with user protection remains a priority.
  - **Workforce Displacement**: Automation may displace certain jobs, requiring reskilling initiatives.

2. **Virtual Reality (VR) and Augmented Reality (AR)**
   Immersive technologies like VR and AR are transforming how people engage with digital environments.

   - **Applications of VR and AR**:
     - **Education and Training**: VR enables simulations for medical procedures, while AR enhances classroom learning.
     - **Entertainment**: VR gaming and AR-enhanced experiences in sports and live events.
     - **Retail**: AR allows customers to visualise products in their homes, boosting e-commerce sales.

- o **Regional Trends**:

  - **USA**: Investment in VR hardware for gaming and industrial applications.

  - **UK**: AR adoption in retail and creative industries, such as fashion and design.

  - **Europe**: Utilising VR for tourism, cultural heritage, and remote collaboration.

- o **Challenges**:

  - **Cost of Adoption**: High hardware costs limit widespread accessibility.

  - **Content Development**: Creating engaging and useful content remains resource-intensive.

3. **Internet of Things (IoT)**
   IoT connects devices, systems, and people to create smarter, more efficient environments.

- o **Applications of IoT**:

  - **Smart Homes**: Devices like thermostats and lighting systems enhance convenience and energy efficiency.

  - **Healthcare**: IoT-enabled wearables monitor patient health in real time.

  - **Industrial IoT**: Sensors optimise manufacturing processes and logistics.

- o **Global Impacts**:

  - **USA**: Leading in smart cities and consumer IoT devices.

  - **UK**: Focused on IoT integration in healthcare and infrastructure.

- **Europe**: Emphasising IoT in renewable energy management and agriculture.

7.1.2 The Growing Role of AI in Digital Business

AI is becoming an integral component of digital business strategies, enabling companies to optimise operations, innovate products, and deliver superior customer experiences.

---

1. **AI-Powered Operations**
   Automation and efficiency are at the core of AI applications in business.

   o **Supply Chain Management**: AI predicts demand, optimises routes, and reduces waste.

   o **Customer Relationship Management (CRM)**: Tools like Salesforce Einstein use AI to enhance customer interactions.

   o **Cybersecurity**: AI detects and mitigates threats in real time, protecting sensitive data.

2. **AI-Driven Innovation**
   Companies leverage AI to design new products and services tailored to evolving market needs.

   o **Product Development**: AI accelerates research and development processes in industries like pharmaceuticals.

   o **Creative Applications**: AI-generated art, music, and design open new possibilities for creators.

   o **Personalised Marketing**: Algorithms recommend products and content based on user behaviour.

3. **Ethical and Regulatory Considerations**
   The widespread adoption of AI raises ethical and legal questions.

- Bias in Algorithms: Ensuring fairness in AI decision-making processes.

- Data Security: Protecting user data from breaches and misuse.

- International Standards: Aligning AI governance across regions for consistency.

7.1.3 Sustainable and Green Digital Economy Trends

The intersection of digital technology and sustainability is driving the shift towards eco-conscious innovation and practices.

1. **Green Technologies**
   Digital tools are enabling sustainable practices in various industries.

   - Renewable Energy Management: IoT and AI optimise solar and wind energy usage.

   - Waste Reduction: Blockchain ensures traceability in recycling and supply chains.

   - Eco-Friendly Manufacturing: 3D printing minimises material waste and energy consumption.

2. **Circular Economy Models**
   A circular economy focuses on resource reuse, reducing waste, and extending product life cycles.

   - Digital Marketplaces: Platforms like ThredUp and eBay promote second-hand goods and recycling.

   - Repair and Resale: Apps like FixIt allow consumers to repair products instead of replacing them.

- o **Sharing Economy**: Ride-sharing and co-working platforms reduce resource consumption.

3. **Global Collaboration on Sustainability**
Digital platforms facilitate international cooperation on environmental issues.

   - o **Open Data Initiatives**: Share climate data to support global research and policy-making.

   - o **Virtual Conferences**: Reduce carbon footprints by hosting events online.

   - o **Crowdsourcing Solutions**: Platforms like Climate-KIC encourage collective action for sustainability.

Conclusion

Emerging technologies and trends offer immense potential to redefine industries, improve efficiency, and address global challenges. From AI's transformative impact on business to the sustainability-driven innovations shaping the future, these advancements hold the key to long-term economic growth and resilience. The next section will delve into **Preparing for the Next Digital Revolution**, focusing on how individuals and businesses can adapt to technological changes and build a future-proof skillset.

7.2 Preparing for the Next Digital Revolution

The digital revolution is an ongoing phenomenon, and its pace continues to accelerate with advancements in technology, shifts in consumer behaviours, and the globalisation of digital markets. To thrive in this dynamic landscape, individuals and businesses must adapt to rapid changes, cultivate future-proof skills, and foster a culture of innovation and creativity. This section outlines strategies for staying ahead in the evolving digital economy.

7.2.1 Adapting to Rapid Technological Change

Technological advancements have a profound impact on industries, reshaping markets, workflows, and customer expectations. Preparing for these changes requires foresight, flexibility, and a proactive approach.

1. **Understanding the Pace of Change**
   Staying informed about technological trends ensures readiness for disruption.

   o **Global Trends**: Technologies like AI, blockchain, and IoT continue to revolutionise industries.

      ▪ **USA**: Emphasis on automation, with AI transforming healthcare, finance, and logistics.

      ▪ **UK**: Focus on tech-driven sustainability and smart cities.

      ▪ **Europe**: Investments in green technology and digital sovereignty initiatives.

- o **Industry-Specific Impacts**:

  - **Retail**: E-commerce innovations like AR-powered shopping experiences.

  - **Education**: Adoption of virtual classrooms and personalised learning tools.

  - **Healthcare**: Expansion of telemedicine and wearable health devices.

2. **Proactive Change Management**
   Preparing for disruption involves strategic planning and the willingness to adapt.

   - o **Scenario Planning**: Develop multiple strategies for potential future scenarios.

   - o **Agile Methodologies**: Foster organisational agility to respond quickly to market changes.

   - o **Employee Engagement**: Communicate the benefits of change to reduce resistance.

3. **Leveraging Opportunities**
   Technological disruption often creates new avenues for growth.

   - o **Early Adoption**: Invest in emerging tools to gain a competitive edge.

   - o **Collaboration**: Partner with tech innovators to co-develop solutions.

   - o **Market Expansion**: Use digital platforms to reach untapped customer bases globally.

7.2.2 Building a Future-Proof Skillset

As technology reshapes job markets, developing skills aligned with future demands is essential for career resilience and advancement.

---

1. **Identifying High-Demand Skills**
   Focus on skills that complement technological advancements and market needs.

   o **Digital Skills**:

   - **Coding and Development**: Proficiency in languages like Python, JavaScript, and SQL.

   - **Data Analysis**: Skills in interpreting data and deriving actionable insights.

   - **Digital Marketing**: Expertise in SEO, social media, and online advertising.

   o **Soft Skills**:

   - **Adaptability**: Navigating change with confidence and creativity.

   - **Critical Thinking**: Evaluating complex problems and developing innovative solutions.

   - **Collaboration**: Working effectively in diverse and remote teams.

   o **Global Perspectives**:

   - **USA**: Demand for cybersecurity specialists and AI engineers.

   - **UK**: Rising need for fintech expertise and sustainability strategists.

   - **Europe**: Focus on green tech and data privacy compliance.

2. **Continuous Learning**
   Lifelong learning is key to staying relevant in a rapidly changing job market.

   o **Online Courses and Platforms**:
      - Coursera, LinkedIn Learning, and edX offer diverse options for upskilling.
      - Specialised platforms like Udacity focus on tech-centric skills.

   o **Certifications**:
      - Google Analytics, AWS Certified Solutions Architect, and PMP certifications boost employability.
      - Regional certifications, such as Europe's GDPR compliance training, enhance market-specific expertise.

   o **Self-Learning Tools**:
      - Use resources like Khan Academy or YouTube tutorials for foundational knowledge.

3. **Networking and Mentorship**
   Building connections enhances learning opportunities and career progression.

   o **Professional Groups**: Join industry associations and online communities.

   o **Conferences and Webinars**: Engage with experts to stay updated on trends.

   o **Mentorship Programmes**: Seek guidance from experienced professionals.

7.2.3 Innovation and Creativity in Digital Business

Innovation and creativity are critical for businesses to remain competitive in a technology-driven economy. Encouraging experimentation and embracing new ideas lead to sustainable growth.

1. **Fostering a Culture of Innovation**
   Create an environment where employees feel empowered to experiment and innovate.

   o **Encouraging Experimentation**:

   - Provide resources for prototyping and testing new ideas.

   - Reward successful innovations and learn from failures.

   o **Cross-Functional Collaboration**:

   - Break down silos to integrate diverse perspectives.

   - Use tools like Slack or Trello for seamless team communication.

   o **Innovation Labs**:

   - Establish dedicated spaces for exploring cutting-edge technologies.

   - Partner with universities or research institutions for knowledge sharing.

2. **Implementing Creative Business Strategies**
   Creativity in strategy development ensures differentiation and market relevance.

   o **Customer-Centric Design**: Develop products and services tailored to user needs.

   o **Storytelling in Marketing**: Use compelling narratives to build emotional connections.

    o   **Agile Product Development**: Iteratively improve offerings based on user feedback.

3. **Adopting Emerging Technologies**
   Leverage new tools and platforms to drive business transformation.

    o   **AI in Decision-Making**: Use AI to analyse market trends and optimise operations.

    o   **Blockchain for Transparency**: Enhance trust in supply chains and financial transactions.

    o   **VR/AR for Engagement**: Create immersive experiences for customers and employees.

Conclusion

Preparing for the next digital revolution requires a proactive approach to technological adaptation, skill development, and innovation. By embracing change and fostering creativity, individuals and businesses can position themselves as leaders in the evolving digital economy.

The next section will focus on **Building a Legacy in the Digital Age**, discussing strategies for long-term financial stability, impactful branding, and digital estate planning.

7.3 Building a Legacy in the Digital Age

In a world increasingly defined by technology and digital assets, building a legacy involves more than traditional methods of wealth accumulation and reputation management. It requires strategic planning for financial stability, impactful branding that transcends generations, and robust digital estate management. This section explores the tools, strategies, and mindsets needed to create a lasting legacy in the digital age, catering to global markets across the USA, UK, Europe, and beyond.

7.3.1 Planning for Long-Term Financial Stability

Financial stability is the foundation of a sustainable legacy. By leveraging digital tools, diversifying investments, and anticipating future trends, individuals and businesses can ensure lasting economic security.

1. **The Pillars of Financial Stability**
   Building long-term wealth requires a multifaceted approach that balances growth, risk management, and sustainability.

   o **Diversified Portfolios**:

      ▪ **Digital and Traditional Investments**: Combine stocks, real estate, and digital assets like cryptocurrencies or NFTs.

      ▪ **Regional Diversification**: Balance investments across markets, such as US tech stocks, UK property, or European green bonds.

   o **Emergency Funds**: Maintain liquid savings to cushion against market volatility or unexpected expenses.

   o **Sustainable Growth**:

- Invest in eco-conscious businesses or green technology initiatives.

- Focus on assets with consistent long-term returns, such as dividend-paying stocks.

2. **Leveraging Technology for Wealth Management**
Digital tools simplify financial planning, tracking, and optimisation.

   o **Budgeting Apps**: Platforms like YNAB (You Need a Budget) and Mint provide detailed insights into spending habits.

   o **Investment Platforms**: Use apps like Robinhood (USA), Freetrade (UK), or eToro (global) to manage diverse portfolios.

   o **AI Financial Advisors**: Robo-advisors like Wealthfront or Betterment offer automated investment strategies.

3. **Global Tax and Regulatory Compliance**
Managing financial stability in a digital economy requires understanding international tax laws and regulations.

   o **Taxation on Digital Assets**:

     - UK: HMRC guidelines on capital gains for cryptocurrencies.

     - USA: IRS rules on NFT and crypto earnings.

     - Europe: Varying VAT and income tax policies for digital transactions.

   o **Cross-Border Investments**: Understand double taxation treaties to avoid overpaying taxes.

- o **Professional Guidance**: Consult financial advisors familiar with global markets and digital economies.

7.3.2 Creating a Lasting Impact and Brand

A meaningful legacy extends beyond financial wealth; it encompasses influence, values, and contributions to society. Crafting an enduring brand ensures your impact resonates across generations.

---

1. **Defining Your Core Values**
   Aligning your brand with authentic values builds trust and loyalty.

   - o **Personal and Professional Alignment**:
     - ▪ Identify principles that guide both personal decisions and business strategies.
     - ▪ Examples: Sustainability, innovation, or community empowerment.

   - o **Storytelling**: Share narratives that highlight your values and journey.

   - o **Global Relevance**: Tailor messaging to resonate with diverse audiences.
     - ▪ **USA**: Emphasise entrepreneurial spirit and innovation.
     - ▪ **UK**: Highlight heritage and tradition alongside modernity.
     - ▪ **Europe**: Focus on sustainability and inclusivity.

2. **Establishing Thought Leadership**
   Position yourself or your organisation as a trusted authority in your field.

   - **Publishing and Speaking**:

     - Write articles, blogs, or books on industry topics.

     - Participate in conferences or webinars to share expertise.

   - **Mentorship and Education**: Create courses, workshops, or mentorship programmes.

   - **Collaborations**: Partner with leading institutions or influencers to amplify your voice.

3. **Building an Enduring Brand**
   A strong brand identity ensures longevity and influence.

   - **Visual Identity**: Develop logos, colour schemes, and designs that reflect your mission.

   - **Consistency**: Maintain uniformity across platforms and communication channels.

   - **Legacy Projects**: Initiate philanthropic or community-driven efforts that align with your values.

7.3.3 Digital Estate Planning and Legacy Management

As digital assets gain prominence, planning for their management and transfer becomes crucial. Digital estate planning ensures your legacy is preserved and passed on effectively.

---

1. **Understanding Digital Assets**
   Digital assets range from cryptocurrencies to social media accounts, each requiring unique management strategies.

   o **Types of Digital Assets**:

     ▪ **Financial**: Cryptocurrencies, online brokerage accounts.

     ▪ **Creative**: Websites, e-books, digital art.

     ▪ **Personal**: Social media profiles, cloud storage.

   o **Valuation**: Assess the financial or sentimental value of each asset.

2. **Creating a Digital Will**
   A digital will outlines instructions for managing and distributing digital assets after death.

   o **Key Elements**:

     ▪ Detailed inventory of assets.

     ▪ Access credentials, stored securely using tools like LastPass or 1Password.

     ▪ Appointed digital executor.

   o **Regional Considerations**:

     ▪ **USA**: State-specific digital estate laws under the Revised Uniform Fiduciary Access to Digital Assets Act (RUFADAA).

- **UK**: Include digital assets in traditional wills to avoid legal disputes.

- **Europe**: Comply with GDPR when transferring personal data.

3. **Legacy Management Tools**
   Technology simplifies the organisation and execution of digital estates.

   o **Platforms**: Services like Clocr and Everplans assist with digital estate planning.

   o **Automation**: Use blockchain-based smart contracts for asset transfers.

   o **Regular Updates**: Periodically review and update plans to reflect changes in assets or laws.

Conclusion

Building a legacy in the digital age requires a strategic approach to financial stability, impactful branding, and meticulous digital estate planning. By embracing these principles, individuals and organisations can create a lasting, meaningful impact that transcends generations.

The final section will summarise key insights from the book, providing motivation and actionable steps for readers to achieve success in the digital economy.

Final Conclusion: Achieving Success in the Digital Economy

The digital economy presents an extraordinary array of opportunities for individuals and businesses alike. From the flexibility of freelancing to the innovation-driven growth of emerging technologies, the digital landscape is a dynamic and ever-expanding frontier. Achieving success in this realm requires a combination of knowledge, adaptability, resilience, and a commitment to lifelong learning. This conclusion synthesises the key insights from the book and provides actionable guidance to help readers excel in the digital economy.

8.1 Summing Up Digital Economy Essentials

Understanding the foundational elements of the digital economy is the first step towards leveraging its potential. This subsection recaps the primary concepts and strategies explored throughout the book.

1. **The Digital Shift**
   The transition to digital platforms and systems has redefined traditional business models and personal income strategies.
   - **Key Takeaways**:
     - **Global Markets**: The USA, UK, and Europe are at the forefront of digital transformation, with increasing adoption in emerging economies.
     - **Business Models**: From e-commerce to subscription-based services, the digital economy thrives on innovation and scalability.
   - **Actionable Steps**:

- Identify areas in your life or business that can benefit from digitisation.

- Stay informed about industry-specific digital trends.

2. **Opportunities Explored**

Each chapter provided insights into diverse avenues for generating income and building wealth in the digital age.

   o **Freelancing and Remote Work**: Platforms like Upwork and Fiverr offer global opportunities.

   o **Investments**: Digital real estate, websites, and apps provide scalable income streams.

   o **Technological Innovations**: Leveraging AI, blockchain, and IoT to optimise business operations.

   o **Real-World Examples**:

      - Case studies from the USA (Silicon Valley startups), UK (fintech advancements), and Europe (green tech initiatives).

3. **The Path Forward**

The digital economy's breadth means there is no single path to success.

   o Explore multiple income streams to diversify risk.

   o Build networks and collaborate with others in the digital space.

8.2 Staying Adaptable and Resilient

Resilience and adaptability are essential traits for thriving in an economy characterised by rapid change. This subsection focuses on strategies to remain flexible and proactive.

1. **Anticipating Technological Change**
   Technological advancements will continue to disrupt industries and create new opportunities.

   - **Adopting a Growth Mindset**:
     - Embrace change as an opportunity for innovation.
     - Stay curious and open to experimenting with new tools.

   - **Future-Proofing Skills**:
     - Invest in learning in-demand digital skills such as data analysis or coding.
     - Focus on soft skills like adaptability and problem-solving.

   - **Global Perspective**:
     - **USA**: Lead in adopting and innovating new tech solutions.
     - **UK**: Maintain focus on ethical and sustainable digital growth.
     - **Europe**: Leverage collaborations for tech-driven regional advancements.

2. **Building Resilience in Uncertainty**
   Resilience enables individuals and businesses to
   navigate challenges and recover from setbacks.

   o **Financial Preparedness**:

      ▪ Maintain an emergency fund to weather
        economic downturns.

      ▪ Diversify income sources to reduce
        reliance on a single stream.

   o **Mental Resilience**:

      ▪ Practise mindfulness and stress
        management techniques.

      ▪ Seek support networks, such as mentors
        or professional groups.

   o **Adaptable Business Models**:

      ▪ Pivot quickly in response to market
        shifts.

      ▪ Continuously refine offerings based on
        customer feedback.

3. **Harnessing Global Trends**
   Monitoring global trends ensures you remain
   competitive and relevant.

   o **Emerging Economies**: Invest in or partner with
     businesses in growing markets like Southeast
     Asia or Africa.

   o **Sustainability**: Align with global efforts
     towards eco-friendly practices.

   o **Remote Work Evolution**: Leverage remote
     tools to expand into international markets.

8.3 Motivation for Future Growth and Learning

Staying motivated and committed to personal and professional growth is key to sustained success in the digital economy.

---

1. **The Importance of Lifelong Learning**
   Continuous education is essential for staying relevant and competitive.

   o **Accessible Resources**:

   - Use platforms like Coursera, Udemy, or Khan Academy for affordable education.

   - Join professional development programmes in your field.

   o **Staying Curious**:

   - Experiment with new technologies or methods in your area of expertise.

   - Attend webinars, conferences, or meetups to broaden perspectives.

   o **Learning Across Borders**:

   - **USA**: Access top-tier educational platforms like edX.

   - **UK**: Engage with institutions focused on fintech and creative industries.

   - **Europe**: Participate in government-sponsored upskilling programmes.

2. **Setting Goals for Growth**
Clear, achievable goals provide direction and maintain motivation.

- o **Short-Term Goals**:
  - Learn one new skill every quarter.
  - Monetise a hobby or passion project within six months.

- o **Long-Term Vision**:
  - Build a passive income stream through investments or content creation.
  - Establish yourself as a thought leader in your niche.

- o **Tracking Progress**:
  - Use tools like Notion or Asana to monitor milestones and adapt plans.

3. **Fostering a Growth-Oriented Community**
Collaboration and networking amplify individual efforts.

- o **Online Communities**: Participate in forums, LinkedIn groups, or Discord servers.

- o **Mentorship**: Seek guidance from experienced professionals and offer support to others.

- o **Global Collaboration**: Work with international teams to gain diverse insights and experiences.

Final Thoughts

The digital economy represents an unparalleled opportunity for growth, innovation, and impact. As you navigate its complexities, remember that success lies not in mastering every trend but in aligning your efforts with your passions, values, and long-term goals. By staying adaptable, fostering resilience, and committing to lifelong learning, you can create a sustainable and meaningful legacy.

Whether you're based in the USA, UK, Europe, or beyond, the principles outlined in this book offer a roadmap to achieving success in the digital age. The journey may be challenging, but with persistence, creativity, and the right strategies, the possibilities are limitless.

Here's to your success in the digital economy!